THINGS
I WANT TO
PUNCH
IN THE FACE

JENNIFER WORICK

REVISED
EDITION

PROSPECT
PARK
BOOKS

The views expressed in this book are solely those of the author, and she means no harm by them. Unless you decide to sue her, in which case she'll want to punch you in the face.

Published by Prospect Park Books
2359 Lincoln Avenue
Altadena, California 91001
prospectparkbooks.com

Library of Congress Cataloging-in-Publication Data is on file with the Library of Congress
The following is for reference only:

Worick, Jennifer.
  Things I want to punch in the face / by Jennifer Worick. — 2nd ed.
     p. cm.
  ISBN 978-1-938849-56-5
  1. American wit and humor. I. Title.
  PN6165.W66 2012
  973.9202'07--dc23
                          2012013640

Second edition, first printing

DESIGNED BY KATHY KIKKERT

Manufactured in the United States of America

THINGS I WANT TO PUNCH IN THE FACE

REVISED EDITION

THE TABLE

Airline Boarding Process
Ancient Grains
Auto-Tune
Backhanded Compliments
Baggage Claim Cock-Block
Bay Shrimp
Beach Makeup and Jewelry
Bizspeak
Black Friday
#BLESSED
Books as Decor
Bucket Lists
Buzzfeed Quizzes
Celebrity Baby Names
Celebrity Fragrances
Chai
Cheetos Dust
Cold-Pressed Coffee
Comfort Shoes
Cosplay
Cross-Pollinated Food
"Curators"
Cyber PDA
Deceptively Bad Produce
Early Birds
Evites
Excessive Punctuation
Family Car Stickers
First-World Problems
Flavor Savers

Food Restrictions
Food Served in Jars
Foodies
The Genius Bar
The Giving Tree
GPS Addicts
Grocery Bag Guilt
Hobbits
Holiday-Themed Clothing
Horror Movie Trailers
IKEA Habitrail
Intentionally Misspelled Titles
It's Versus Its
Jazz
Kids' Songs
Knighted Celebrities
Last Swig of Beer
Limp Handshakes & Wimpy Hugs
Long Toenails
Lumbersexuals
The Magic 8 Ball
Malapropisms &
    Mispronunciations
Man Caves
Mercury in Retrograde
Mimes
Mirrorless Dressing Rooms
Mixologists
Molly Ringwald's Prom Dress
    in Pretty in Pink

OF PUNCHES

Motel Art
Mr. Darcy
Nail Art
Naked Pregnancy Portraits
Namaste
New Year's Eve
New Yorker Cartoons
Non-Prescription Eyeglasses
Obligatory Standing Ovations
Pajamas as Outerwear
Parents Who Give Their Offspring
    Names All Starting with the
    Same Initial
Parking Hogs
Passwords
Patchouli
Paypal
Peach Schnapps
Penis Names
People Who Blab on Red-Eyes
People Who Don't Believe in TV
People Who Stop at the Top of
    Escalators
People Who Watch All the Movie
    Credits
Polar Bear Plunges
Pollen
Precious Moments
Prolific Dead People
Quadraboob and Uniboob

Renaissance Faires
Restaurants That Don't Put Salt
    on the Table
Scrabble
Seat Hogs
Shoeless Households
Sidewalk Hogs
Silk Flowers
Special-Occasion Fleece
Spinning Beach Ball
Staycations
Steampunk
Stripper Brows
Sunglasses on the Forehead
Talking About Yourself
    in the Third Person
TED Talks
TOMS
Topping Off Coffee Without Asking
Twenty-Minute Coffee Prep
TYPING EMAILS IN ALL CAPS
Unsalted Nuts
Utilikilts
Vanity Plates
White Pizza
Windsocks
Year-Round Christmas Decorations
Yoga Pants
Zumba

INTRODUCTION

Welcome to the new edition of *Things I Want to Punch in the Face*, a non-rose-colored-glasses view on life. See, things irk my shit on a daily basis. Alone, they are not a big deal, but add to it a stressed gal with a short fuse and you get—you guessed it, Einstein!—something I want to punch in the face.

So without further ado, I present my latest take-no-prisoners take on life's little annoyances.

For instance, I'd like to smack down waiters who top off my coffee without asking. I might have just gotten it to the right temperature and blend of cream and sugar when they come along and fill up my decaf cup with regular joe while I'm eyeballing the dessert menu. I'm the boss of me, not someone with a nametag! I want to punch these presumptive knobs in the face.

I'm not gonna lie: This isn't a new phenomenon. It's easy to say that I'm as bitter as black coffee because of the economy or my perpetually single status or an extra ten pounds. I could talk about the crappy eight days that prompted me to actually start recording my peeves in ridiculous detail. But if I'm honest with myself, and with you, things bug me on a daily, if not hourly, basis. They always have. I'm generally a good-natured, dare I say happy, person, but I'm also human. Like Alanis Morissette, a fly in my Chardonnay isn't something I'm going to celebrate. (Unlike Alanis Morissette, I know the definition of "ironic.")

But I just might bitch about it, maybe even write about it. And I'm not alone. You probably have had moments or days where you wanted to kick something, scream, or burst out laughing at the absurdity of lumbersexuals or white pizza. Maybe you even wanted to punch something in the face. *Hard.* Now's your chance, at least vicariously. And hey, if you really do have to clean something's clock, why not aim your fist at this book cover? I aim to please, and so I hope you'll be as pleased as punch reading these rants as I was when I smacked them down.

GUIDE TO THE PUNCHES

ANNOYING
like a mild rash

AGGRAVATING
like a black eye

DISGUSTING
like an open sore

TOXIC
like acid reflux or IBS

PERMANENTLY DAMAGED
like my patience

AIRLINE BOARDING PROCESS

PUNCH RATING 👊 👊 👊 👊

I recently was flying out of Seattle when I realized just how low I ranked on the food chain of travel. I wasn't flying first class. Or business class. And I didn't have gold, silver, or aluminum status. I wasn't a member of the military, or even wearing camo cargo pants ironically. I didn't have small children or a feeble grandparent in tow. I wasn't disabled, on crutches, or zooming around in one of those motorized La-Z-Boy scooters.

And no, I wasn't sporting a Russell Wilson Seahawks jersey. Which on that day moved you to the front of the pre-boarding line. It didn't matter that I checked in twenty-three hours and fifty-nine minutes before our flight. I clearly was not part of any cool kids' club.

Can it really be called pre-boarding when ninety percent of passengers are locked and loaded by the time they announce Zone One? Airlines want us to pay for upgrades so we can board earlier and, more importantly, feel as though we're part of an elite group, the Star-Bellied Sneetches of the skies.

Here's an idea: Maybe they should shift it to *post*-boarding. Board all of the seemingly normal, deodorant-wearing folks first and then call for the dregs. Wearing patchouli? You can take the seat in the very last row. Lump all the Chatty Cathys together and seat them in the same row. Got a pupu platter of dietary issues? You get to board only after the gate attendant flogs you with a bunch of lacinato kale that you get in lieu of the snack pack. Carrying a shit-ton of computer equipment so you can rock some in-flight spreadsheets? Enjoy sitting between the 6'7" dude in front of you and the inconsolable toddler who likes to kick behind you.

Or maybe the airlines should just go all *Lord of the Flies* at the

boarding gate and let us fend for ourselves. Armed with my conch shell as my only carry-on item, I'll be elbowing my way to the exit row in short order, Russell Wilson jersey or no.

ANCIENT GRAINS

PUNCH RATING

QUESTION: WHAT IS AMARANTH?

A. *A city in the Holy Land where Jesus reputedly lost his sandals*

B. *A flowering bulb similar to Amaryllis*

C. *The latest celebrity baby name*

D. *A gluten-free ancient grain*

> **FACT OF THE MATTER**
>
> ⟶ There may be more celiac disease and gluten sensitivity today because wheat has been bred to be hardier, shorter, and better growing. Haven't we learned anything from the royal family?

You probably have a frenemy who sings the praise of a gluten-free lifestyle while you're tucking into Eggs Benny at brunch, so you know the answer is D. You also know that ancient grains and their grassy-eyed acolytes need to be ground into a fine flour.

Along with spelt, ancient grains like quinoa and teff sound more like onomatopoeia describing a punch to the gut than a digestible alternative to wheat. And Quaker Oats had to go and get on the picky foodie bandwagon. They just rolled out quinoa granola bars. What's next? Millet Pop Tarts? Kamut Krunch cereal?

Ancient-grain devotees think there's some magical quality associated with something so old it rated a mention in the Bible. Newsflash: That prophet in Ezekiel eating millet? It didn't give him the key to eternal life. Back in the BC days, they suffered high infant mortality, plagues, short lifespans, and a host of problems that a bowl of wheat berry porridge couldn't fix. Now, if these foods had antibiotic-infused kernels that would keep my UTIs in check or heal a wound, I'd be the first in line to cook up this stuff for consumption—or a poultice.

Ancient grains may be healthy, but they're not the way to the promised land. That's what kale is for.

AUTO-TUNE

I can't sing. I learned this a long time ago, when folks used to turn around and stare at me during Mass when I was trying to rock "Amazing Grace" or "Ave Maria." My tone-deafness was driven home during high school. Whenever the spring musical rolled around, I was relegated to the chorus or the comic relief cameo—both decidedly non-singing roles—and asked to mouth along to the group numbers.

I had my "come to Jesus" moment about my vocal chords long ago. God blessed me with so many other talents that it'd just be greedy to wish for the voice of Aretha Franklin. And we all know that greed is one of the Seven Deadly Sins.

> **FACT OF THE MATTER**
> ✤ The path to musical hell is paved with good intentions—auto-tune was initially created by an Exxon engineer who was developing methods to interpret seismic data.

I accept my shortcomings. So too should singalings like all those Real Housewives who can't carry a tune. Money can't buy you class...or a good singing voice. And shame on folks like Usher, Bon Iver, and wil.i.am, who actually can sing. Back away from the audio processor or I might have to auto-turn my fist toward your voicebox.

BACKHANDED COMPLIMENTS

PUNCH RATING 👊 👊 👊 👊 👊

I can't get over how good you look.
You're so lucky. If I ate like you, I'd look like a house.
You don't look happy in that.
That sweater is...interesting.
I just think it's a little young for you.
It's a hat, all right!
You're more of a "street smart" kind of guy.
You're not the kind of girl guys date; you're the kind of girl they marry.
You're so evolved...for a man.

> **FACT OF THE MATTER**
> ✦ There's a real name for this—asteism is a "genteel" way of deriding another. Here's my genteel response: Go away...please.

As a perfectly bred broad, let me be perfectly clear.

The backhanded compliment really should be called a backhanded cutdown, because there's absolutely nothing complimentary about these sorts of comments. Worse than actual criticism, they drip with condescension, as though I am too thick to pick up on what you're really saying. Oh, I get it. And it sucks. You suck.

Spit it out and say what you mean, or keep your rude trap shut. If this dress makes my skin look like a rotten cantaloupe, I'd sorta like to know. If you think I said something inane, keep it to yourself. With loads of etiquette options in front of you, don't secretly delight in choosing the road less mannered. Don't rationalize away the passive-aggressive comment by believing you're refraining from saying what you really think. Instead of demonstrating tact, you're just putting the ass in class.

And in case that was unclear in any way, that's not a compliment.

BAGGAGE CLAIM COCK BLOCK

Are you way more important than everyone else?
Is your luggage made of solid gold?
Are you smuggling someone across the border in a steamer trunk
     without air holes?
Did your water just break?

If you answered "yes" to any of these questions, fine. You might suck dead bear, but I'll give you a pass at the baggage claim carousel. If you answered "no," you must need me to fly my fist in a northerly direction toward your face.

Lemme tell you why.

When a flight lands, I try to hightail it out of the airport. Sometimes I'm forced to check a bag, so I haul ass from my arrival gate, only to find myself jockeying for position around the baggage carousel while I wait for my Samsonite to tumble down the conveyor belt. You'd think I'd be so flippin' happy to be off my flight and out of its Lilliputian seats that I'd just be content to feel my limbs again.

Uh, no.

The flightmare continues as I elbow my way through chuckleheads in pleated khakis or gamey business suits with phones clipped to their belts, parents who are wrangling several unruly kids hopped up on M&Ms, and reunited couples engaged in serious tonsil hockey. Who the fuck knows if my bag made it to my destination, since I can't see the conveyor belt, let alone get to it. Asshats of every kind queue up against the carousel, forming a Hands Across American Airlines bond that I can't break through. When a waste of space scores a bag, he doesn't remove it from the fray. No, he usually sets it beside himself to create an additional hurdle for me to trip over/kick the shit out of when I finally spy my bag amid the golf clubs, checked car seats, and floral tapestry suitcases littering the conveyor belt.

Then there are the families.

If you want to queue up like the von Trapp Family Singers,

so be it. Just be aware that I'm going to use my carry-on bag and my laptop case to box your ears like a monkey rocking the cymbals. Find your roller bag now, bitch. I don't think that red ribbon you tied onto the handle is gonna help you.

BAY SHRIMP

PUNCH RATING

I love shrimp, I do. So the description of "Bay shrimp," found on menus at crusty country clubs everywhere, sounds delightful to me, like the shrimp had been surfing some tasty waves off the Baja Peninsula before they were netted.

So, so off base.

Rather, Bay shrimp are teeny-tiny versions of a grown-ass shrimp. These embryos look like they should have had more time in the water to gestate and become fully cooked. As they are, they look like they should be sent off for stem cell research instead of dressed with ranch dressing or made into seafood salad.

In lieu of a scoop of Bay shrimp, I'll take two to three grilled prawns, thank you very much. Drop that pink larvae on a decomposing body so it can get to work, or ship it off to some fisherman so it can be used as bait for something more worthwhile.

> **FACT OF THE MATTER**
> ✦ Bay shrimp are smarter than they appear: They are an indicator species and are sensitive to overfishing, changes in temperature, pollution, and fluctuations in salinity.

BEACH MAKEUP AND JEWELRY

PUNCH RATING 👊 👊 👊

As the temperatures soar, I beeline to the beach. But instead of cooling off, my blood really starts to boil when I spot tantards tricked out in full-on makeup and their entire jewelry box. Even if you happen to be a Kardashian sister or are filming a reality show, back away from the waterproof eyeliner and the gold bangles.

Wearing the complete cosmetic cornucopia—foundation, blush, bronzer, eye shadow, eyeliner, mascara, lip liner, lipstick—is going to clog your pores, particularly if you add

> **FACT OF THE MATTER**
> ✦ It's no small comfort to know that a bronzed babe's gold and silver will become tarnished when exposed to salt water.

sunscreen into the mix. And when you wear a tangle of necklaces or a fistful of rings, you're adding tan lines, dulling your baubles, and risking their loss or damage.

Oh, and you look fekking dumb. It's like you're trying too hard. Frankly, you look desperate. Sorry to put sand in your Spandex, but the beach is a place to chill and let your hair down. It's not the place to show off your new Shimmer Brick and tennis bracelet.

Step away from the MAC and the Maybelline, and leave the ghetto gold back at the beach house. Real beach bunnies have the confidence to embrace the elements and their natural beauty. I learned that from *Baywatch*.

BIZSPEAK

PUNCH RATING 👊 👊 👊

Our business needs to grab the low-hanging fruit.

Take that idea offline and put it in the parking lot.

Let's have a meeting to drill down into that idea and then dogfood it to the company.

We need more bandwidth to support the drop-down menu on the landing page.

Schedule a meeting next week for a masterminding session on monetizing our site.

How can we get to yes?

> **FACT OF THE MATTER**
> ✦ The Franklin Planner is named after Ben Franklin, who apparently had personal organization on his long list of accomplishments.
>
> **FACT OF THE MATTER**
> ✦ International Talk Like a Pirate (ITLAP) Day is September 19, matey.

Um, are you developing a new language? You should know that the only cool language to invent is pirate speak, matey.

If you insist on talking nonsense in a bid to sound like you know what you're doing, I'm going to have to take out my phablet and beat you, restructuring content without boundaries from the top down. It's time for a deep dive so I can get granular with my ire. Oh, you want to brand yourself, you say? Pull down your flat-front trousers so I can go old-media on your ass and brand you with a red-hot poker. That's my kind of growth hacking.

This particular SOW is in my wheelhouse.

BLACK FRIDAY

PUNCH RATING

I'm sure you'll agree with me that "Black Friday" evokes some sort of horrific tragedy, such as a massacre or a deadly plague or the end of days. And indeed, just for an extra 15 percent off, people risk exposure to H1N1, unvaccinated children in germ-ridden shopping carts, and women who will cut you with their coupon if given a chance.

Am I the only one who thinks this scenario is absoloonly nuts?

> **FACT OF THE MATTER**
> ✦ Our founding fathers would be so proud—the term "Black Friday" was coined around 1960 in that cradle of democrassy, Philadelphia.

This excruciating day has been called "Retail S&M." If I want a little slap and tickle, I sure as shit am not going to look for it in the aisles of Walmart on Whack Friday. God invented the internet so we can avoid hot strip-mall messes and crowded parking lots in favor of leftovers and online shopping. And oh yeah, porn. Lots of porn.

#BLESSED

PUNCH RATING 👊

Well, duh.

Way to state the obvious, Einstein. Of course we're blessed. We live in a privileged society with fluoride in our tap water, computers and flatscreen TVs in every home, organic chickens in many pots, access to health care, and Beyoncé. While many of us don't need to, we shop at Goodwill because it's cool.

> **FACT OF THE MATTER**
> ✦ The number sign (#) has been called the "hash symbol" in some countries outside of North America, which led to it being introduced on Twitter in 2007 to tag topics.

Adding a hashtag that telegraphs your gratitude and piety wastes eight characters, and it clues in your tweeple that you are an unoriginal windbag who's humblebragging your sweet-ass life as the chosen one (Gwyneth) or trying to cover up the fact that you're just happy to be here (Lindsay). Either way, it sounds insincere.

Put the #blessed to rest. Swap it out with something that conveys what you're actually thinking. Instagramming your engagement ring? #couldabeenbigger. Tweeting about the French toast your kids surprised you with? #chokingdowngluten. Commenting on an unflattering throwback Thursday photo that a childhood friend posted and tagged you in? #paybackisabitch.

I guarantee that you'll get retweeted. #amen.

BOOKS AS DECOR

"The more that you read, the more things you will know.
The more you learn, the more places you'll go."
—Dr. Suess

You are what you read. At least that's what I hoped back when I was rocking Dr. Seuss as a five-year-old or Jane Austen as a thirtysomething lady.

But some folks don't care what they read. They use books as props, buying or renting them

> **FACT OF THE MATTER**
> ✦ Forget the white edges of a book's pages. Gilding is where it's at. An expensive treatment, gilding serves as, yes, decoration, but thanks to the metallic gold leaf, it also protects the book from such environmental issues as acidity and dampness.

by the foot from companies that will select them by color, style, or subject for you. I've even seen a company that sells blocks of books that have been glued together, apparently to make it easier to move when dusting. And heck, they'll always be lined up perfectly.

I just threw up a little in my mind.

My bookshelves offer a snapshot into my history, my interests, my (now vomit-covered) brain. They reflect my intellectual DNA (which is why I haven't cottoned to ebooks yet), and it's hard to imagine viewing my books only as squares and rectangles of color to accent my home. I've even seen books arranged spine IN, to create a swath of white along the shelves. I was confused. How are you supposed to figure out which book to read? Oh, right. They aren't there to be read. They're there for me to knock some *Sense and Sensibility* into your head.

BUCKET LISTS

PUNCH RATING

I'm all for living your life to the fullest (like Bon Jovi says, "I just wanna live while I'm alive"), but there's something about putting your dreams and aspirations in a bucket that seems just plain wrong. Maybe if it was called the Silk Purse List or the Safety Deposit Box List or the Goody Drawer List, I could choke the idea down. But bucket? Can't we find a worthier receptacle for our unfulfilled desires?

I get it. Kick the bucket and all that. Riiiiight. When I'm in my death throes, am I expected to seize up and randomly punt a bucket that just happens to be sitting next to my deathbed? What, was I just digging up potatoes or mopping the floor? When I'm about to buy the farm, I don't envision myself as an indentured servant.

> **FACT OF THE MATTER**
> ✦ The film *The Bucket List* grossed upward of $175 million worldwide. On my bucket list? Punching director Rob Reiner in his meathead.

Fuck the bucket. Live each day like you are dying. Don't lie in bed, don't ask for ice chips, and don't check crap off a list. Go out, eat your way through all the lobster in Maine, have a lot of boom-chicka-boom-boom sex, be present in every single moment, and lose the suck-it list. If you don't, I'll have no choice but to fulfill my lifelong dream of clocking you nine ways 'til Sunday. It's right up there with skydiving and riding a bull named Fu Manchu.

BUZZFEED QUIZZES

PUNCH RATING

I thought I was so smart, managing my social network feeds. I opted out of seeing a certain frenemy's posts (the "Gwyneth Paltrow of Seattle"—you'd hide her too). I blocked Oregon Trail, Farmville, and every other bullshit Facebook game. But I can't seem to shake the quizzes—oh the horror, the quizzes. They started out benignly enough. I took a two-minute break to find out if a Buzzfeed quiz could deduce,

based on my language and pronunciation preferences, which part of the country I'm from (spot on). But then the inanity mounted. Which *Breakfast Club* character/breed of dog/Dr. Who are you? Which Hogwarts house do you belong in? Which Disney cat should be your pet? Are you more Lorelei or Rory Gilmore? Really, what kind of insight can be gleaned from finding out which celebrity man bun I am?

Admit it, you hate yourself for taking the bait (I'm the Leonardo DiCaprio man bun, by the way). That's two minutes of your life that you can't get back. That shit adds up. *Five hundred twenty-five thousand six hundred minutes, how do you measure, measure a year?* The creators of *Rent* weren't envisioning 262,800 quizzes that you'll forget about as soon as you answer question ten. You could have read a great article, left a loved one a voicemail, told someone off in the library parking lot, worked on a crossword, or gone number two. Better alternatives to these quizzes lurk everywhere, even in the crapper.

CELEBRITY BABY NAMES

PUNCH RATING

Pop quiz: Which of these are actual Hollywood baby names?
a. Ikhyd
b. Summer Rain
c. Audio Science
d. Pilot Inspektor
e. All of the above

You guessed it, being all smart and shit, that the answer is "All of the above."

I don't hate the players, I just hate the names. I'm happy to have these kids grow up and join my posse. Kal-El and Moxie Crimefighter can knock down my haters. Hermes is destined to be my personal shopper, and Sage Moonblood my nutritionist.

Kids have enough problems without insecure yet narcissistic parents saddling them with a nutbar name. Why not let them discover who they are, rather than assigning them a name that's sure to seal their fate?

> **FACT OF THE MATTER**
> ❖ The name of Jason Lee's son, Pilot Inspektor, was inspired by the song "He's Simple, He's Dumb, He's the Pilot," by the band Grandaddy. I suppose it's better than the alternative of Simple Dumb Lee.

Ikhyd sounds like an exotic animal that can roam the plains alongside an okapi. Jermajesty and Banjo are gonna get their asses kicked up and down the playground. And even *I* feel fucked just thinking about Audio Science.

For shits and giggles, let's change your names and see how you like it. From here on out, Kal-El's daddy Nic Cage is going to be called

Lex Loser. Rachel Griffith (Banjo's mom) is hereby dubbed Accordion Fold. Christina Aguilera birthed Summer Rain (not to be confused with Lil' Kim's little one Royal Reign), so I think it's more fitting to change her name to Spotty Showers. Audio Science's mom, Shannyn Sossamon, can be tagged as Exhibit A and be used as a test subject in a research experiment.

> **FACT OF THE MATTER**
> + Barbara Hershey boarded the crazy train early on, naming her son Free in 1972. Clearly this came at a cost; Free changed his name to Tom when he was nine years old.

And, finally, Robert Rodriguez, since you are a repeat offender (Rebel, Racer, Rocket, Rogue—ridiculous), I'm going to give you a special moniker; I'm thinking Reduce Reuse Recycle.

CELEBRITY FRAGRANCES

PUNCH RATING 👊 👊

Britney, J Lo, and the Biebs keep churning out stinkers, and I'm not talking about their singles. Divas keep littering cosmetic counters with hiddy scents that are not "reminscent of classic Hollywood allure," like Forever Mariah Carey promises, but rather call to mind "poorly dressed skank" or "botched boob job."

When we whiff "Fantasy," are we supposed to forget about Britney's barefoot excursions to gas station bathrooms, let alone her cooch flashing, head-shaving, paparazzi-attacking antics? Are we supposed to feel like we've unlocked "The Key" to smelling great when spritzing Justin Bieber's scented hair mist over our locks?

I can smell the marketing bullshit from here, which I guarantee is celebrifree airspace. Even if a scent doesn't induce the gag reflex, do you really want a bottle of Fergie's Outspoken embarrassing your dressing table? Stop pouring money into Kim Kardashian's foul empire and Jessica Simpson's ginormous Louis Vuitton bag and just say no to eau de ho.

> **FACT OF THE MATTER**
> ✦ The sweet smell of success: Perfume "makers" Avril Lavigne and Derek Jeter can thank Elizabeth Taylor for kickstarting the celeb fragrance movement; White Diamonds still stands as the best-selling celebrity fragrance in the United States.

CHAI

PUNCH RATING 🖐 🖐 🖐

Is it tea? Is it coffee? Is it just plain woo-woo pretentious? What the fuck are you, chai?

If you're not living in or touring India, chances are you are drinking a powdered version of this spiced milk tea, or even a bastardized chai/coffee hybrid. For instance, I just discovered to my dismay that a dirty chai doesn't involve extra olive juice, but a shot of espresso.

But it's not just the chai itself. It's the knobs who drink it. When sipping on this strange brew, these exotic creatures somehow feel enlightened and superior, much like I imagine Tom Cruise and his Scientology cronies feel after a good L. Ron Hubbard jamboree. Doctoring up their chai with a dollop of soy milk and a soupçon of cardamom, these wannabe Siddharthas eat, pray, and love throwing the stinkeye at my mocha choca latte and silently judging, all the while say-

> **FACT OF THE MATTER**
> ✦ Indian chai acts as a natural digestive.
>
> **FACT OF THE MATTER**
> ✦ *Chai* (or *cha*) is the generic word for tea in many countries.

ing crap like "namaste, my friend" to my face while reaching for their heart center.

I want to punch these nirvana-in-a-cup-seeking sultans of swill in their third eye, until they're blind.

CHEETOS DUST

Like Shakira's hips, Cheetos don't lie. When viewing the orange mist in my car, on my clothing, on my couch, it's clear that there's been a high Cheetos count lately. And if you were to turn on a black-light or spray some Luminol in my pad, you might see an occasional orange splatter pattern. Clearly, something really bad happened on the right side of my couch.

While I love to put away orangefood at every and any opportunity, I don't really like the radioactive goo that cakes my fingers. (Okay, that's a lie. I just

> **FACT OF THE MATTER**
> ✦ Cheetos' flavor and composition can vary by geographic region. If you find yourself in Asia, sample Savory American Cream in China and Strawberry Cheetos in Japan.

hate the damage it does to my surroundings when I don't lick my fingers lickety split.) As I got out of the car recently, my pal gave me a strange look. She then attacked me, wiping me down and beating my clothes until a cloud of orange rose up around me. Thank God. Without her delousing, people on the street would have thought I had come out on the wrong side of a fight with a Tang canister.

I can't punch Cheetos in the face because it will only exacerbate the problem. The only thing to do is to throw some cold water on this all-unnatural snack food…literally. Either that, or I'm going to mix it with some lotion, create a faux-spray tan, and dress up as an Oompa Loompa.

COLD-PRESSED COFFEE

PUNCH RATING

Just when I thought coffee culture couldn't get any more precious, cold-brew coffee shows up to the delight of coffee snobs and the dismay of pretty much everyone else.

The hot drink equivalent of small-batch spirits, cold-brew (or cold-pressed) coffee is produced by steeping coffee grounds in chilled or room temperature water for 12-plus hours.

Hipsters far and wide are queuing up for this brew, which makes the coffee less bitter (while jacking up my own bitterness) because the coffee beans never make contact with actual hot water. This coffee concentrate can then be heated up and added to water or milk for a supposedly transcendental caffeine experience.

Cold-brew coffee has been popping up all around my town, Seattle, with some bars even offering the coffee on tap or in growlers. This translates into lumbersexuals everywhere coming in their artfully distressed jeans.

I hate to throw cold water on this, but if you need a cuppa joe to get your rocks off, you might want to rethink things. A sweet cup of coffee is a wondrous thing, certainly, but it will never beat out a sweet piece of ass. Sip on that.

> **FACT OF THE MATTER**
> ✦ The inventor of the paper coffee filter, German housewife Melitta Bentz, experimented with various methods and materials before striking gold with blotting paper. When her filtered coffee met with enthusiasm, she set up a business in 1908. She got a patent, and the rest is a century of delicious grounds-free coffee.

COMFORT SHOES

We've put a man on the moon and created fabrics with UV protection. We've cloned a camel, for crying out loud. So I'm frankly puzzled as to why cushioned and supportive shoes invariably give you Frankenfeet. Bouncing along in personal flotation devices, you might feel fantastic, but you look like you've been in a car accident, what with those casts encasing your hooves and all.

Dansko, Birkenstock, Merrell, Easy Spirit, Earthies, and, ugh, Crocs—y'all are the red-headed stepchildren in my shoe wardrobe. You're part of the footwear family but should remain out of sight if you know what's good for you. Soles are bulbous, footbeds

> **FACT OF THE MATTER**
> ✦ Birkenstock has a long-storied history shodding feet in the Vaterland; Johann Adam Birkenstock was registered way back in 1774 as a shoemaker. I hope someone smacked him in the face with a cork footbed.

stanky, and uppers rounded, wide, and clunky. Sensible with a side of suck, these travesties manage to look like clown shoes while simultaneously announcing that you've just given up.

If your designers can't cook up a sleek approach to comfort and cushioning soon, I'm going to dig out my red Dansko clogs and inflict a bit of blunt-force trauma. Did I just put my foot in your mouth?

COSPLAY

PUNCH RATING 👊 👊 👊

My name is Jennifer Worick and I am a nerd. A Coke-bottled, bookworm, comic book–collecting, Nerdist-loving nerd. But apparently, I'm not a cool one, because I have never been to Comic-Con. And I don't have a closet filled with *Logan's Run*, Xena, Bellatrix Lestrange, or *Jem and the Holograms* costumes. I don't even own any wigs. And I'm okay with that.

See, I'm also a grown-ass person. Every day isn't an opportunity to indulge in a flamboyant case of arrested development. I get it, Stormtrooper, I get it. You were a kid with *Star Wars* sheets who doesn't have a girlfriend and wants to take out your agro-bro feelings under a guise of white plastic while trolling for a slave Leia. And sexy Uhura with your skirt up to there, I know you had braces and a case of crippling shyness as a teen, so now you're making up for lost time and looking for a Mr. Spock to call your own.

> **FACT OF THE MATTER**
> ✦ It all started with Comic-Con, founded as a comic book convention in 1970 and, like Tribbles, soon expanding exponentially. Now it attracts upward of 130,000 men who long to be Luke Skywalker and women who really wish they had an invisible jet.

Take the lead from kids, who save the serious costuming for Halloween. Dressing up for every conference for comic books, pinball, sci-fi, manga, Magic the Gathering, videogames, and Trekkies co-opts what should be *one* special day and, frankly, throws you into the same sorry bunch as steampunkers and Ren Faire enthusiasts. You just have more interesting eyewear. So go to a galaxy far, far away—wrap your knitted scarf around your neck, step into your TARDIS, and find some Daleks looking to exterminate a Time Lord.

CROSS-POLLINATED FOOD

PUNCH RATING 👊 👊 👊

Some things, like peanut butter and chocolate or mac 'n cheese, are a match made in epicurean heaven. Then there's the cheeseburger pizza. Contrary to popular Pillsbury belief, it's not the best of both worlds. It's neither a cheeseburger nor a pizza.

I'm all over innovation. But when it comes to food mash-ups, not all creations are created equal. For every cronut, there's a Paula Deen frankenfood waiting to kill you with cholesterol. While I can tuck into a tater tot casserole like nobody's business, certain foods have no business commingling. Pick a lane, taco

> **FACT OF THE MATTER**
> ✦ Paula Deen's Lady Brunch Burger features a hamburger patty tarted up with a fried egg and bacon and bookended by two Krispy Kreme glazed doughnuts. Burgers and doughnuts are two foodstuffs that should never, ever meet on a plate.

pie. Stop waffling, waffle sandwich. Tacos and Doritos are beautiful things on their own — why did Taco Bell have to jump the shark with Doritos Locos Tacos? And McRib, you're just McWrong. Although I gotta hand it to McDonalds for having the 'nads to introduce a boneless, and maybe even meatless, McRib sandwich.

What's next? Chocolate chicken wings? A sausage-link latte? Tilapia crème brûlée? It's time to order up a large fist with a side of ire, and rain Pepto Bismo–laced punches down on these match-made-in-hell misses.

"CURATORS"

PUNCH RATING

When strolling the galleries of museums both grand and intimate, I am always grateful for the discerning eye and expertise of curators, even if I don't always fancy the art itself. In college, I interned at a terrific museum in Washington, DC devoted to art by women. I went on behind-the-scenes tours of other museums ranging from the National Gallery to the Corcoran, and I sat down with curators for brown-bag lunches to learn about what they do. I even helped take a Frankenthaler off the wall.

Respect, y'all.

But sadly, the ranks of actual curators have been breached and sullied. Just like anyone can start a blog, print up one hundred Moo cards, and call themselves a professional writer, so too can some yambag "curate" a list of cured meats for a regional magazine or a collection of sunglasses or yoga pants for Piperlime.

> **FACT OF THE MATTER**
> ✦ The word "curator" comes from the Latin *curator* ("one who has care of a thing, a manager, guardian, trustee"), from *curare* ("to take care of"), and from *cura* ("care, heed, attention, anxiety, grief"), none of which indicate that a bearded guy should ever get to be called a curator for just really, really liking pork belly.

So you eat a lot of sausage and like to shop. Do you have a PhD in anything remotely relevant? Is there any standard that makes you a bona fide expert in anything other than being obnoxious? And then there's the trend to call employees "content curators." Call me crazy, but in my day, that was an editor. So go ahead and offer your top-ten list or opinion freely and often, but don't call yourself a curator. The only thing you're qualified to select and collect is my ire.

CYBER PDA

PUNCH RATING

I think it's sweet that you love each other, I really do. I'm happy to see status updates, tweets, and blog posts about your courtship, engagement, and wedding. Not only can I handle it, I'm heartened by it.

But my support of your relationship does not mean I want to be slimed with your cyber makeout sessions, your oversharing, and those sweet nothings all goddamned day. Tweeting about how much you miss your flaxen-haired beauty—even though you've only been apart an hour (which I know because you tweeted that, too)—or updating your Facebook status to detail what an incredible night you had with your Sweetpea or Huggy Bear

> **FACT OF THE MATTER**
> ✦ As a term of endearment, "honey" dates back to ancient Greece. Sweet. You know what's not so sweet? Dropping "honey bunny" bombs toward your significant other all over Facebook.

makes me, in this order, 1) roll my eyes, 2) choke back my breakfast, and 3) want to share the love. Specifically, I dream of playing Cupid, pulling out a crossbow, and piercing you through the heart, or at least your fingers.

Take a note from Shakespeare: Speak low if you speak love. In other words, keep it in your pants and send your true love an email. We don't want to see that sap. That's what porn, Jane Austen novels, and Reese Witherspoon movies are for.

DECEPTIVELY BAD PRODUCE

PUNCH RATING

Scene: Kitchen. Mouthwatering smells are emanating from all corners of the room. In the center, an impeccably dressed, radiant hostess prepares to cut into

an avocado. Guests are due to arrive in minutes.

Ten seconds later: "Are you #$%^&*$#Q@% kidding me?" The hostess surveys the decay that has reared its fugly head on her cutting board.

The avocado is rotten.

As you can imagine, this romantic comedy just became a tragedy.

When the farmers' market is closed during winter, I shop at the grocery store. I take my time in the produce department, thumping, sniffing, and pinching, trying to suss out freshness. Apparently, I suck at this.

I pick out avocados that seem destined for my delicious guacamole, only to cut into them and find them rotten. I peel an orange and find it devoid of any juice. Tomatoes, watermelon, and all manner of fruits find their way into my kitchen and then into the compost pail. Don't even mention a mealy apple in my presence.

Aside from the disappointment, these douchebag foodstuffs cut into my budget. I invested in that jicama and it totally hosed me.

A good piece of fruit can transform my day from mediocre to magical, and conversely, one bad apple can spoil my lunch…and the whole damn day. I want payback. I want to beat black-hearted produce into a bloody pulp.

EARLY BIRDS

PUNCH RATING 👊 👊

Whenever I have unhappily stumbled into an office or coffee shop at 7 a.m., I see a flock of smug early birds silently congratulating each other for being such productive, rarified members of society. These chipper toolboxes are one step away from developing a secret handshake. This sort of self-satisfaction would be irksome enough, but add to that their silent disdain for anyone who sets their alarm for sometime after sunrise and they really make me want to flip my shit.

Dude, so you get to your desk at the ass-crack of dawn. You are the first one to turn off the security alarm. You regularly meet with your trainer at 5:30 a.m. You have special alone time with the boss. Whoopadeedoo! The only thing this means is that you go to bed at 9 p.m. You climb under the covers before the sun goes down, which is not something to pat yourself on the back about, unless you're a farmer.

Don't give me the stinkeye when I roll in. Don't even hint that I don't work hard for the

> **FACT OF THE MATTER**
> ✦ The poster child of early birds, larks are diurnal, meaning that they at their liveliest from sunrise to sunset.

money. I usually toil away until I turn off the lights long after midnight, so eat my alarm clock. We have different schedules, different rhythms that suit us. It doesn't mean that your day is any longer or more fruitful than mine. It just means that you're a judgmental fuck who drinks decaf after 2 p.m.

The best part of waking up is piping hot Folgers in your face.

EVITES

PUNCH RATING 👊 👊 👊

I'm going to make a bold statement: Evites are the downfall of etiquette as we knew it.

Evite burst onto the scene in 1998 and quickly became part of the fabric of our lives, hooking us with its ease of use and transparency. And once the site reeled us in with cutesy-wootesy birthday and cocktail-party templates, we got lazy.

⊰ Too lazy to send proper invitations. I just heard today about an Evite that was sent out for a small memorial service for a classy, elegant woman. She deserved better. She deserved hand-written invitations on 100-pound vellum. If you're having a housewarming party for everyone you know, pick a festive design and Evite the shit out of your shindig. If you're hosting an intimate get-together to mark a significant event, care enough to send the very best. Get thee to a Hallmark, y'all.

⊰ Too lazy to explore other options for online invitation tools that aren't littered with ads and a slow user interface. I only find out about sites like Paperless Post when friends more adventurous than me invite me to their birth ritual or moving-abroad party.

⊰ Too lazy to RSVP properly or at all. Evite notifies guests on the invite list by sending emails, but it doesn't include the event details.

So people often don't even bother to click through to the actual information, let alone reply. And if they do reply, they get a chance to sit on the fence with a "Maybe." Good etiquette mandates that you either respond with a "Yes" or "No," not an "I'll try to come but I might be on a deadline or out of town." I call bullshit.

And yet, I can't bring myself to just say "No." The allure of being able to peruse the guest list in advance is just too irresistible. Is my former lover planning on coming with a Plus One? Are my favorite people opting out, leaving me to make stilted chitchat with that horribly dull man who never ever asks me a question about me? Is that snotty fashionplate coming? If so, I'll have to step up my sartorial game, even though it's a picnic on the beach. Evite helps us to make important decisions like these regarding party attendance without peppering the host with inappropriate questions.

So am I going to finally kick Evite to the curb? "Maybe." But I know for sure that for my next soirée, I'm indulging my love of stationery and loading up on some letterpress invitations.

EXCESSIVE PUNCTUATION

PUNCH RATING

I get it!!! I really do!!! Srsly!!!!!!!!!!!!!!!

I know you're excited or scared or confused or slumped over the keyboard so your ear keeps hitting the question mark key. There's no need to drive home the point by slapping me in the face with punctuation marks or poking me in the eye with those goddamn extraneous exclamation points.

I'm a big advocate of everything in moderation and yep, that applies to my semicolons. Ever since high school, I figured there was a perfect way to express anything through words. Words. Not punctuation. Spend more time conveying what you mean through language, please, and leave those poor, defenseless exclamation marks alone. What did they ever do to you?

F. Scott Fitzgerald said, "Cut out all those exclamation marks. An exclamation mark is like laughing at your own jokes." Word, Fitz, word. Can you imagine the difference it would

> **FACT OF THE MATTER**
> ✦ An exclamation point or exclamation mark is also called a bang and a dembanger, the latter of which I'm thinking should be my drag queen name.

make if he had thrown in one or several exclamation points to his otherwise gorgeous WASPy text, such as when Gatsby describes Daisy?

The original: "Her voice is full of money."

The icky: "Her voice is full of money!!!"

A beautiful observation becomes the sort of squawking, self-congratulatory promise that a Shamwow ad delivers. Less is more. Period.

FAMILY CAR STICKERS

PUNCH RATING

Wow, you're a family? Get out! I would never have guessed that you have a full house by the minivan you're driving.

The decal equivalent of a "Life Is Good" T-shirt or Vera Bradley backpack, customized family stickers are just another way to crow about your awesome functional family. Honestly, wouldn't a holiday photo with matching red sweaters do the trick?

Maybe it's just that my ovaries have gone to seed, but this 2.0 version of a Baby on Board sign isn't going to engender warm, fuzzy feelings in me. Rather, this smug stick figure art makes me want to stick something else to this family, namely a bumper sticker over your two-dimensional family that reads GANG OF BORE.

> **FACT OF THE MATTER**
> ✦ Baby on Board signs were first unleashed on the US market in 1984, peaked the next year, and were mocked by 1986, with parodies cropping up like "Mother-in-Law in Trunk." Can we please get on board with kicking family car stickers to the curb?

FIRST-WORLD PROBLEMS

PUNCH RATING

After meticulously planning a two-week vacation, my luggage did not arrive with me. I had to wait around my friend's apartment for a good day and a half, stewing in the same clothes I'd started my journey in, nine time zones away.

Poor me.

Then I looked at the bright side. 1. I was in Paris. 2. I was staying for *free* in an apartment that was *two* blocks from the Eiffel Tower and whose French doors opened onto a balcony

> **FACT OF THE MATTER**
> ✦ How come we never hear about second-world problems? When this three-world model was created back in the day, the Second World included the Soviet Union, China, and their allies— i.e., Communist countries.

upon which Audrey Hepburn would have been right at home. I may have been washing my panties out in the sink, but I was in Paris. In other words, *un problem du premier monde.*

First-world problems are everywhere. *"Should we go to the beach today or just hit the resort pool instead? You know I hate getting sandy." "I'm in a pickle. My Swiss au pair isn't arriving until a week after the kids finish preschool." "One of my resolutions is to purge my stuff this year and simplify and streamline. I just have way too many clothes, shoes, books, CDs, computer gear, train memorabilia..."*

I sympathize, I really do. But a first-world problem that actually needs to be addressed is our collective lack of perspective and self-awareness. I'm sorry you weren't able to snag those heirloom tomato seeds, and it sucks that your metabolism has plateaued and you can't lose those last five pounds. But every time you get PO'd, take a breath and think of a third-world problem. Nothing like Ebola or a lack of clean drinking water to make the long line at Chipotle suddenly bearable.

FLAVOR SAVERS

PUNCH RATING

Frankly, I'm stumped. What's the thought process behind the crumb catcher that's also known as a soul patch? I wish I was a passenger on that train of thought....

It'll make me look handsome, slimmer, younger, cooler, douchier...

Clearly, there has to be intent behind the soul thatch, since it's groomed and shaped to within a hair of its life. Are you trying to lengthen your face? Did you need an arrow to find your mouth? Did you slip with the razor and have to keep on pruning? Whatever the case, I have to break it to you: Dude, you're sporting a bikini wax on your chin.

Be it the Frito or Dorito, you've got a landing strip on your face. Runways belong at O'Hare, not on your nearly hairless mug. Only Bruce Springsteen can pull that shit off, and, while he was born to run, he's still skating on thin ice. Embrace the Brazilian. It'll only hurt for a minute. However, if you keep that thin dead line on your puss, you're in for a world of pain as I wax, thread, sugar, and shave your face, all the while withholding the Ibuprofen. Just call me a flavor shaver.

> **FACT OF THE MATTER**
> ✦ Jazz musicians of the 1950s and '60s sported soul patches, giving me yet another reason to punch jazz in the face, specifically the chin.

FOOD RESTRICTIONS

PUNCH RATING

Going out to eat with friends or family is one of life's greatest pleasures. But it turns into an exercise in frustration and mortification when that loved one has food restrictions. Being gluten-free is child's play in the face of folks who are dairy-free and nut-free, avoid sugar in any form, prefer their water filtered, and are currently avoiding eight major foods as part of an elimination diet.

This is when I'd like to eliminate them. Or disappear into the floor of the restaurant, after giving the server a sympathetic look and a massive tip.

We all thought Meg Ryan in *When Harry Met Sally* was a high-maintenance diner. While she might be the patron saint of picky eaters, her request for salad dressing on the side seems downright quaint today. It's great that as a society we've evolved to the point that we can eliminate major food groups. It's a genuine first-world problem. The Irish weren't in a position to cut out starches when the famine hit, for feck's sake. And I bet a starving child in Burundi would be more than happy to down that lobster mac 'n cheese you just poo-pooed, dairy, gluten, and shellfish sensitivities be damned.

If you don't want to eat something, navigate toward something else on the menu or stay home and roast an organic chicken. Don't ask the chef to change a dish he or she spent considerable time perfecting. And don't broadcast your food issues to the table. This type of extreme self-care just comes off as an attempt to pull focus from what really matters—that lobster mac 'n cheese. I'm packing Prilosec.

FOOD SERVED IN JARS

PUNCH RATING

I love Anthropologie, I do, but I don't want to *eat* there.

These days, restaurants—so precious that I want to squeeze their whitewashed and reclaimed-wood cheeks—are squeezing all sorts of tasty cakes, casseroles, and puddings into Mason and Ball jars.

Adorable.

But what looks like a saccharine craft project becomes another kind of project, as I try to scrape, pull, and otherwise extract all of the tasty goodness out of the jar and into my piehole with a spoon or fork that doesn't have the same curvature. Serve my molten chocolate cake or soft-boiled egg with a spatula, if you insist on stuffing it into a jar better suited for jam.

Let my food breathe on the plate, so I can breathe a sigh of relief.

> **FACT OF THE MATTER**
> ♦ The Mason jar was invented and patented in 1858 by a Philadelphia tinsmith to preserve food at home. I don't suspect he ever figured it would be used to house everything from chicken pot pie to tiramisu.

FOODIES

PUNCH RATING

Don't sniff it, don't eyeball it, don't comment on how it's plated like a pagoda or a Zen garden, don't detail the 39 steps it took to make it, don't start comparing it to the meal you had at El Bulli back in the day, and don't complain about the new chef while alternately giving me his culinary CV.

I don't want to hear it. I just want to eat it.

I love food as much as the next person. I like food the way Homer likes his doughnuts.

But a food snob I am not. You'll never find me asking whether my Copper River salmon was gill-netted and bled and dressed on site. I'll never lift a fiddlehead fern and wax rhapsodic about hunting the zenmai in East Asia during a trip with Anthony Bourdain. I'll fork that fern and put it where it belongs: my belly.

Don't put nettle pasta on a pedestal, put it in your piehole. After all, it's food. You're supposed to eat it, not dissect it.

Sometimes, I just want to eat a box of mac 'n cheese, and not the Annie's kind. And I don't need you to tell me how to zest it up with Emmentaler and linguiça. Don't take the comfort out of my food or I might have to bust out the mandoline and create a new dish of hurt.

> **FACT OF THE MATTER**
> ✦ According to The World's 50 Best Restaurants website, the number-one restaurant in the world in 2014 was Denmark's Noma. Mmm, Nordic cuisine.

THE GENIUS BAR

PUNCH RATING

ME: "Why do I want to punch the Genius Bar in the face?"
SIRI: "I have a fishbowl punch located on the menu at the Genie Bar.
    Do you want directions?"

I'm a longtime Apple-only user. I know a few key commands, I can solve most glitches on my own, and some friends even ask me for Mac advice. I used to believe all this was sort of a "na-nu

> **FACT OF THE MATTER**
> ✦ Genius Bars have been stroking egos and touch pads since 2001; they are headed up by a Lead Genius, who should take off his glasses and wait for my iPunch.

na-nu" secret handshake into the cool kids' club. Heck, I even wear interesting eyewear, for the love of Steve Jobs. *Prescription* eyewear, bitches.

But when I mosey up to the Apple Store's Genius Bar, my illusion/delusion is shattered. I'm not nerdy cool. I'm a tool. My only consolation is that I'm beta-lame, while everyone ahead of me in line is a 2.0 tool (in fact, they might be cyborgs). I have a lot of time to observe these bearded, Apple Watch–wearing creatures in their natural habitapp, seeing as my Casio just went from 3:00 to 3:45—Cupertino time—while I wait for assistance on a stool clearly imported from the distant future.

It doesn't take a genius to figure out that Apple is shamelessly trying to stroke my ego, whispering in my ear like a 21st-century iAgo. There's no need to make me feel like a Mensa member just because I belly up to the bar; my IQ score did that for me in fifth grade. Bitches.

THE GIVING TREE

PUNCH RATING

I can't decide who's the bigger asshole: the tree or the kid.

In thinking about this since my childhood (I wanted to punch Shel Silverstein's classic in the face even then), I have never figured out what all the precious fuss was about. While some claim this book is about unconditional love, to me it smacks of a cautionary tale heard over and over again in twelve-step programs. In addition to being a playmate (branches to swing on), a protector (shielding the kid from harmful rays), a provider (offering up its fruit for food, branches for a house, and trunk for a boat), and a stool (finally a stump), the Giving Tree is a sap. Plus, the tree is female, which makes her continual sacrifice to this knob even more annoying and questionable.

Might I suggest that this parable serve as a lesson to all the other anthropomorphic trees and shrubs out there? Set some boundaries, learn to say no, and get your Serenity Prayer on. Accept that you can't change greedy, thoughtless little shits, muster up some courage to change your behavior and drop an apple on his head, and get wise to his ways. That's the path to happy, joyous, and tree.

> **FACT OF THE MATTER**
> ✦ Spike Jonze wrote and directed *I'm Here*, a 2010 short film based on *The Giving Tree*. The two main characters are robots, which sounds WAY better than a tree and a boy.

GPS ADDICTS

PUNCH RATING

"What are you doing?"
"I'm putting the restaurant we're going to into my GPS."
"Um...it's a half-mile down this road."

Shuttle and cab drivers, go right ahead and go crazy with the positioning systems. Maybe the route from the airport won't be quite as circuitous (and pricey) with some help from above. On a long road trip, go ahead and bust it out. I'm all for things that make life easier. But some geographically challenged chumps seem to be using GPS to find their own ass.

You've lived in this neighborhood for years, Lostco de Gama. You don't appear to have suffered a crushing blow to the head resulting in temporary global amnesia. So why on earth do you turn to a bossy machine to get anywhere and everywhere?

> **FACT OF THE MATTER**
> ✦ The most popular GPS voice belongs to a slightly bossy and therefore hot Australian woman.
>
> **FACT OF THE MATTER**
> ✦ GPS is maintained by the U.S. government; it became fully operational in 1994.

Why do you require assistance to drive in a straight line, Christopher Coldumbass? High school geometry must have been a real bitch. Word problems probably sent you into the fetal positioning system.

Why do you need a disembodied automaton with an Australian accent to tell you what to do? That's what a dominatrix is for, duh. And I'm right here in the passenger seat, ready and willing to tell you where to get off, if you get my drift.

GROCERY BAG GUILT

PUNCH RATING

I'm a bad citizen of the earth. I admit it. When I walk out the door, I don't always know that I'm going to wind up at the grocery store, and consequently, I might not have any sort of bag, basket, bowl, or tray with which to carry my groceries home. So sue me (or charge me that annoying five cents per bag that you're itching to).

I feel like a total hosebag when I skulk—bagless—toward the cashier to ring up my snacklets. I start apologizing to the employee, who really couldn't care less if I take home eleven plastic bags.

My carbon footprint is pretty damn small even if my hooves

> **FACT OF THE MATTER**
> ✦ In 2009, the U.S. International Trade Commission reported that the nation uses 102 billion bags each year.

are a healthy 9 1/2. I use public transportation, my pad is tiny, I turn out the lights, I recycle.

I use plastic bags as trashcan liners and paper bags for recycling, and yet my guilt persists, which seriously pisses me off. And there are a lot of green assholes—grassholes—ready to pass judgment on me and my bag stash. I've seen the stinkeye in the checkout line, believe me.

I have taken steps toward assuaging my guilt. Over the past year or so, I've accumulated quite a few market bags. I bought one I thought was cute, I was given a couple, and I even made an adorable bag as a craft project for a book. But do I remember to take them with me?

Nay.

So I'm left with a wad of plastic bags and a serious resentment toward my inner grasshole. Something must be done: dropkicking my grocery-bag guilt to the curb…into a recycling bin, of course.

HOBBITS

Fuck Middle Earth.

There, I said it. I'm suffering from Hobbit fatigue and I don't care who knows it.

The Hobbit is a children's book, which makes sense because so many Hobbiterations suffer from acute arrested development. Tolkien's books attract

> **FACT OF THE MATTER**
>
> ✦ In Middle Earth, the word "Hobbit" comes from the *Rohirric* word Holbytla, which means "hole-builder." Let's hope they dig one now and live there for a long, long time (because, you know, they live much longer than humans).

Wizards of the Coast–playing, utilikilt-wearing, shaggy Peter Pans who live in their parents' basements and whack off while fantasizing about feeling up Galadriel.

The tale of Bilbo Douchebaggins was recently chronicled in a big-screen trilogy, and nerds everywhere rejoiced once again, having been in mourning since the *Lord of the Rings* trilogy concluded. Here's the thing, geeks—you aren't fringe clusters of bespectacled virgins playing Halo and talking about prime numbers. You and your culture have taken over. You have a place as a programmer waiting for you at Microsoft. You don't need a waistcoat and hairy prosthetic feet to feel like you're part of a quirky band of brothers. You may not be the 99 percent, but you are the 3.14159 percent.

Back away from the shire and the cosplay before I lead you to the Misty Mountains and leave you there. Let's see how you like being barefoot then.

HOLIDAY-THEMED CLOTHING

PUNCH RATING

We get it, Star-Spangled Dumbass, it's the Fourth of July. With the pop-up fireworks stands, numerous picnic invitations, and my calendar, I had an inkling.

While I think a jaunty scarf or baseball cap in our nation's colors can set off an outfit and proclaim your Independence beautifully, I take issue with clothing purchased solely for a holiday. Whether it's an emerald-green outfit befitting a leprechaun, a Quacker Factory sweater adorned with jack-o-lanterns or Christmas trees, or a Valentine's Day heart attack, seasonal clothing is as gauche as wearing a white gown to someone else's wedding.

> **FACT OF THE MATTER**
> ✦ Even the most elegant (i.e., British) among us make a misstep now and again. Witness Mark Darcy's reindeer jumper in *Bridget Jones's Diary*. His parents gifted it to him, and apparently he really, really loved them, bad taste and all.

And, American Idiot, tricking yourself out head to toe in red, white, and blue $5 Old Navy or Target clothing that was made by one-armed Asian toddlers isn't the way to convey your national pride.

That's what illegal fireworks are for, Thomas Feel-Some-Paine. That's just common sense.

HORROR MOVIE TRAILERS

PUNCH RATING 👊 👊

I'm home, minding my own business. The front door is locked, the windows secure. I'm wearing my jammies.

And then, unexpectedly, I'm violated. By my television.

I might be innocently watching the nightmare that is the 56th cycle of *America's Next Top Model* or a grisly autopsy on *CSI* when the show cuts to a commercial. Sigh. Instead of a Cover Girl ad, it's a god-damned horror movie trailer. A young girl is running in the woods, presumably away from a psychopath or the not-so-Steadicam that's hunting her down. In just two minutes, I hear screaming and I see duct tape, knives, guns, sweaty unshaved faces, moody lighting, fear, choppy editing, a microwave....

My heart is racing and I'm seriously disturbed.

It's coming from inside the house. Like Drew Barrymore in the opening sequence of *Scream*, I can't escape. It's bad enough that *Friday the 13th* forever screwed my chances for a fear-free camp-

> **FACT OF THE MATTER**
> ✦ Part of the reason TV commercials seem louder than the program you were just watching is that you were probably listening to human voices, which don't have as much range as music and slasher audio effects. The horror, the horror.

ing trip, but now I have to be afraid every time I reach for the remote. The obvious solution is to quickly turn the channel or turn off the TV before I punch it in its liquid crystal display. Fuck that. These trailers make me mad as hell and I'm not going to take it any more.

It's time to turn the tables on my tormentors. I'm going to enlist that demon chicklet in need of a deep conditioner and a comb from *The Ring* to help. Samara could crawl into the TV and magnetize anything that triggers my gag reflex.

IKEA HABITRAIL

PUNCH RATING 👊 👊 👊

Confession: My home is lousy with IKEA. But it's not for any love for the brick-and-mortar store (or *butik*, to the Swedes out there).

Nr.

As I seek out my Malm bureau, I realize I should have picked up a bag of meatballs from the giant cooler in the Swedish Food Market so I could leave a trail. Even with the help of the signage that sprouts around every corner like skinny Kvart lampposts, I'm lost in the mousetrap, or should I say mousetråpp?

The IKEA habitrail is rivaled only by Gaylord Opryland Hotel, which still comes in as a distant second. They should just put a giant hamster wheel and a water dropper by the entrance and make it official. Clogged with kids hopped up on lingonberries and couples quarreling over the merits of Vanvik vs. Floro bed frames, the aisles of IKEA are sure to bring on a headache faster than the time it takes to fill up your cart with crap that's not on your list. Instead of monster bags of tealights, IKEA should fill the endcaps with bins of ibuprofen. Ädvil is a name that would be right at home in this Swedish funhouse; just don't forget the umlaut.

> **FACT OF THE MATTER**
> ✤ IKEA is an acronym using the initials of the founder's name, as well as the farm he grew up on and his hometown. Instead of determining your porn name, what's your IKEA name? (Initials, farm, hometown.) Mine would be JAWLS, or maybe JÄWLS.

INTENTIONALLY MISSPELLED TITLES

PUNCH RATING 👊 👊 👊 👊

When asked by a national magazine why she named her album *The Dutchess* and not the proper "duchess," Fergie had this to say (hint: She's not from the Netherlands): "The spelling is different because I didn't want people who didn't know how to say it to call it 'the Douche-ess.'"

It gets better.

"I thought, 'Let me dumb-ify it a little bit.' Sometimes you smarten things up and get more clever with words. It's fun to go the other way, and it's always nice for people not to expect as much from me."

> **FACT OF THE MATTER**
>
> ✦ Quentin Tarantino had a few explanations about the spelling of *Inglourious Basterds*, saying once that it's a "Basquiat-esque touch." Um, no. It's a yambag touch. Jean-Michel was known for graffiti, not illiteracy.

Um, sweetcheeks, sorry to break it to you, but after "My Humps," I wasn't exactly expecting you to play chess with Bill Gates. But I did hope that you'd proofread the title of your CD.

Is it street to be stupid? Is it in vogue to be a low-forehead asshat? Call me nutbar, but why not use your celebrity to educate and elevate your audience? Why ya gotta be an inglourious basterd?

This sort of widespread dumbing-down interferes with my pursuit of happiness and makes me want to engage in mortal kombat. I guess the only way to deal with these spellwreckers is to call in some Merriam and Webster to knock some sense—or at least an ability to spell the title of their album or film correctly—into them.

IT'S VERSUS ITS

PUNCH RATING

I could go on about my disdain for the wrong use of "there," "they're," and "their," or "hear" and "here," but what really drives me batshit crazy is the improper use of "its" and "it's." There is no reason that it's confusing. Seriously. If you fuck this up regu-

> **FACT OF THE MATTER**
> ✦ In the UK in 2009, the Birmingham City Council banned apostrophes from all public addresses, using the logic that no one understands how to use them properly. Way to pander to your less-gifted citizens.

larly, there is something wrong with you, you had a shitty teacher in junior high, or you just don't care, which is almost worse. Language is sacred to me. When you mangle "it," you figuratively shit all over my Strunk & White with your grammatical apathy.

This is all you need to remember: If you can say "it is" instead of "it's" and it sounds right, then you should use an apostrophe. "It's" is a contraction and should ONLY ever be used that way.

For example:
It is raining men = It's raining men = Perfectamundo.
The rain in Spain falls mainly on it's plain = Just plain wrong.

If you need any further help remembering this, I can go Pavlov on your remedial English ass and inflict a little conditional response with my fist every time you bungle "its" usage. That should remedy the situation, don't you think?

JAZZ

PUNCH RATING

In general, I like to know where I'm going, be it a drive, a project, or a piece of music. Jazz fills me with agita. I don't know when it's going to end, and I don't know what the squirrely fucker is going to pull next.

I have to say, I'm kind of blue about this. Unlike handlebar mustaches and mimes, I want to like jazz. I want to don a beret and sit in a dark club, nodding my head and saying things like, "yeah, man" and "dig that smooth groove." I used to think I wasn't smart enough to get jazz. Now I feel as if all the cool kids know the secret Herbie Hand(cock)shake and left me out of the Felonious Monk Memorial Clubhouse.

> **FACT OF THE MATTER**
> ✦ Duke Ellington said, "By and large, jazz has always been like the kind of a man you wouldn't want your daughter to associate with." Um, it's actually the music I don't want to associate with.

This only fuels my anger, which is swelling to the point where I want to give the Dave Brubeck Quartet a serious time out and inflict some damage on David Sanborn's reed. Scat needs to scram. You dig, Dizzy?

KIDS' SONGS

"Baaaaackpack, backpack!"

"Hot dog! I've got the rhythm in my head."

"There were ten in the bed and the little one said, 'Roll over, roll over.'"

Clearly, there are many problems with the above scenario (TEN in the bed? Are we in a Dickens novel?); however, the biggest beef I have is that I can't get the mother-lovin' song out of my head.

As much as I tried to sing "Doncha wish your baby was hot like me?" to my goddaughter, it's the wheels on the bus that go round and round in my head. A friend once instructed me to hum the *Entertainment Tonight* theme whenever I got stuck in an endless loop of song suckage. Happily, this worked for wrong songs from Sisqó, the Baha Men, and a musician ex-boyfriend, but kids' songs are more insidious. They appear innocent on the surface, which makes them all the more sinister (think of what happened to baby-face Anakin Skywalker if you need a cautionary tale).

This will not do.

Since shouting some 2 Live Crew or other material offensive to Tipper Gore's ears might stunt a toddler's growth, I propose that for every Wiggles or

> **FACT OF THE MATTER**
> ✦ While it seems to have been lodged in our hippocampus since birth, the earliest printing of "Row, Row, Row Your Boat" with lyrics and music as we know it goes back much further, dating to 1881.

Little Einstein song we have to jazz hands our way through, they get to suffer the decidedly non-hummable sounds of early *American Idol* auditions. That's some aural poop that will never get stuck in anyone's cerebral sandbox.

KNIGHTED CELEBRITIES

PUNCH RATING 👊 👊 👊 👊

Hey you, with the fancy title and doodad pinned to your chest: Did you rescue a damsel in distress? Pull a sword out of a stone? Do battle in the name of the crown?

No? What's that, you say? You played a vixen on *Dynasty* and bear responsibility for introducing shoulder pads to the 1980s? Showed your power by "Stayin' Alive" on the airwaves in 1977? Make expensive handbags that only royalty and Oprah can afford?

When Joan Collins, the Brothers Gibb (who really are Knights in White Satin), and Anya Hindmarch are getting knighted, call me a dissenter. It seems like the Queen is handing out Grand Cross stars right and left. Does she pick up the medals in bulk at Costco?

Sir Bono sounds like a fancy cut of bone-in meat at a steakhouse. Damn, I mean, Dame Kylie Minogue apparently nabbed the Order of the British Empire for her "services to music." David Beckham, OBE? More like OMG. I think Henry Winkler is the bomb, but I don't see how the "thumbs up" merits a knighthood for the Fonz.

Your Majesty: I know it's fun to have some hip playmates who will show up at state functions wearing inappropriate clothing and serenade you with a rousing rendition of "Can't Get You Outta My Head," but you don't have to buy your way into the cool-kid crowd. Unless one of these celebrities figures out how to slay a dragon—and I'm not talking about kicking a mean drug habit or getting a full sleeve tattoo of Grendel—put down the medals and pick up the phone. I'm sure they'd come for the night.

LAST SWIG OF BEER

PUNCH RATING

An ice-cold beer is the perfect complement to so many things: fish and chips, Polish sausage, my left hand. Couple my thirst for a cold one with slow service and my miserly nature, and you'll find me drinking every last drop from the bottle.

Herein lies the problem.

The last swig of beer is always, without fail, a disappointment, a letdown akin to hooking up with an ex or tracking down your high school crush. It's warm—you could heat a room with it. It's flat, like a soda that's been sitting on the counter for three days. And it's sour… like backwash. That last ill-advised sip leaves your mouth tasting faintly of hurl. In other words, it's puke-flavored broth. I don't know about you, but this isn't the taste I want left in my mouth at the end of the night, if you get my drift.

This afterwaste is going to get an afterlife. Being thrifty and shit, I'm pouring the dregs of every last bottle and can of PBR/MGD/IPA/BFD into a vat and repurposing this pukewarm swill to make bread or shampoo. Flat beer may bring me down, but damn if it doesn't fluff up my hair.

> **FACT OF THE MATTER**
> ✦ PBR is so named because it was inexplicably deemed "America's Best" at the 1893 Chicago World's Fair.

LIMP HANDSHAKES & WIMPY HUGS

PUNCH RATING

I dig a strong handshake. Mine is a point of pride, and I always extend my hand with intention and strength. I don't get folks who place their hand in mine and sort of just leave it lying there, so I can hold their flaccid mitt. If I wanted a dead fish in my hand, I'd be down at the waterfront flirting with the fishmongers. If you're going to shake my hand, press the flesh like you mean business. I don't care if you have sweaty palms, raggedy cuticles, or aph-

> **FACT OF THE MATTER**
> ◆ No surprise, but a University of Alabama study found folks with limp-wristed handshakes to be more neurotic and shy than their firm-handed counterparts. I would also add lame to the list.

ephobia. I do care if you washed after peeing. If you can't muster up the energy to grip my hand and give it a few pumps, rest assured I'm going to curl that hand up and steer it in the direction of your face. So much for your fear of being touched. Touch my fist, friend.

And if you're going to hug me, press your body against me properly so I can hook my leg around your ass. That's just good form. Don't lean in and pat me on the back without actually making contact with me. It either indicates that 1) I smell (which is clearly ridiculous), 2) you are afraid of my boobs (which is possible), or 3) you hate the idea of human contact. Embrace intimacy, embrace me. I won't bite (unless I really like you).

LONG TOENAILS

PUNCH RATING

Riddle me this, ladyhawke: Are you trying to pick up small rodents during flight?

Because that's the only reason I can imagine that you're clicking along with those talons looping over your flip-flops like a grounded raptor.

Isn't there a point where life and practicality might suggest that you whittle those can openers off? Like, for instance, when

> **FACT OF THE MATTER**
> ✦ Fingernails and toenails are made of keratin, a tough protective protein. This protein is also found in the hooves and horns of different animals, which may be why someone with long toenails resembles one of the raptors in Jurassic Park, clicking around on the kitchen tile.

putting on a closed-toe shoe? Or your basic bipedal walking?

Clip, saw, file, chew, and otherwise hack those claws off or I'm going to have to sic an actual bird of prey on your ungroomed hooves. Their beaks can clip those nails in no time.

LUMBERSEXUALS

Everything old is new again. When I think about the resurgence of canning or Michael Keaton's performance in *Birdman*, I can get behind this. But the lumbersexual isn't content with honoring the past; he has to turn it into artisanal, curated preciousness. Authenticity is swapped out for hipness. It's not enough for a lumbersexual to find a favorite barbecue joint and lick his fingers in spicy bliss. He has to amass a carefully curated collection of regional hot sauces and a deep well of knowledge on the best way to smoke a pork shoulder. And then create a YouTube video demonstrating the process using his GoPro and Final Cut Pro.

How do you spot a lumbersexual, a subset of the modern hipster male? Well, if you live in Portland, just walk to the nearest corner. But for other regions of the country, a primer:

Above the waist, it's all 1871 up in there. They might as well be in the Big Woods, tapping maple trees with the Ingalls family. Beards are so long that they look like levers. Just pull on one and watch the lumbersexual turn into a human nutcracker, one that could, in his facial hair, actually store nuts—organic roasted nuts dusted with curried sea salt, obvs.

Then there's the plaid. Don't get me wrong; as a former Catholic schoolgirl, I cotton to plaid the way Taylor Swift seeks out high-waisted swimsuits. But I don't want to wear it six days a week, only swapping it out on laundry day for that graphic tee that says "I shot the serif."

Below the waist, the lumbersexual is completely of the moment, outfitted either in spendy jeans so skinny he had to channel his inner teenage girl, laying on the floor to get them zipped, or in saggy-ass Goodwill denim that gives his suspenders a *raison d'être.*

Either way, it's neither attractive nor alluring. I don't want to get wit you or even hang with you; I just want you to direct me to the nearest barn raising or the best creek for gold panning. So get on your fixed-gear bike—the one with no brakes—and head for the hills. Find someone else

> **FACT OF THE MATTER**
> ✦ I blame Paul Bunyan. The granddaddy of the modern lumbersexual began as an oral tradition of North American loggers, accompanied not by a fixie but by Babe the Blue Ox. It's a wonder the Decemberists haven't written a song about him yet.

to talk to about your Whiskeytown bootlegs. Roll up your flannel shirt sleeve and show off your forearm tattoo of the butcher cuts of a pig to someone who cares about the difference between hocks and trotters, because I'm way too busy plucking, shaving, and waxing. Hair removal never gets old.

THE MAGIC 8 BALL

PUNCH RATING

Screw you, Magic 8 Ball, and your "Better not tell you now" coyness. You think you're so superior, telling us all what's what with your terse responses. Would it hurt you to give me an affirmative one of these days? I mean, I do my part. I focus, I shake, I beg, I plead, I stroke your smooth exterior. "Reply hazy try again," "Cannot predict now," and "Don't count on it" may be truthful, but would it hurt you to throw me a bone once in a while? Everyone knows that polite white lies are just good form if the truth is going to hurt. You don't see me telling you "My sources say you suck," do you? No, I keep it to myself, because I'm classy that way.

> **FACT OF THE MATTER**
> ✦ The twenty-sided die inside the Magic 8 Ball sports ten positive answers, five negative, and five noncommittal, which just makes my pissoffedness "Without a doubt" all the greater when I keep getting my hopes dashed.

You might as well just say "He's just not that into you" or "Poverty is in your future," stab me in the heart with a sharp point of your fickle icosahedral die, and be done with it. Stop prolonging the agony, or better yet, give me an "It is certain" or a simple "YES" every now and then, you smug ball of jackassedness.

MALAPROPISMS & MISPRONUNCIATIONS

PUNCH RATING

I've been a stickler for language since I was in seventh grade, which means I've been one persnickety fuck for decades. I try to tamp down my know-it-all-ness when a friend mangles the mother tongue (luckily I surround myself with smart people) but nevertheless, I internally cringe when someone busts out a malaprop or mispronounces a word.

There are words and phrases that have been around since the dawn of the Oxford English Dictionary, or at least since we've been alive. It's harder to forgive the repeated slip of the tongue. That makes me think you just don't give a rat's ass.

Or it makes me think that you're George W. Bush. Dear Mr. Presidon't, I'm so glad I no longer have to hear dimwitticisms like "We need an energy bill that en-

> **FACT OF THE MATTER**
> ✦ "Malapropism" traces its roots to Mrs. Malaprop, a character in a 1775 play, *The Rivals*, by Richard Brinsley Sheridan.

courages consumption" or "We cannot let terrorists and rogue nations hold this nation hostile." Dude, you went to Yale, for fuck's sake. Could you at least *try* to appear intelligent?

To me, the most oft-misused and ear-bleeding offense is "irregardless." When I worked at a publishing company, we editors would roll our internal eyes every time the owner threw that out in a meeting. Let me reiterate: I worked at a PUBLISHING company. Dude should have known better. Better yet, dude should have been punched in the face.

And if I hear someone bust out "nuculur," I'm going to mushroom cloud all over them, even if they were once president.

MAN CAVES

You man, me woman. I get it. It's not that hard to figure out our differences. You shave, I wax. You like *Dirty Harry*, we dig *Dirty Dancing*. But when it comes to portioning off areas of the house, I don't see why you XYs need your own space to watch sports or porn or whatever it is you do in there. You don't need a separate hole to crawl into when you are discovering fire or sharpening tools. That's what the garage is for, Encino Man.

> **FACT OF THE MATTER**
> ✦ To sound crazy smart, throw around "speleology" when entering a man cave. It's the study and exploration of caves.

And your male room shouldn't be where the wagon-wheel coffee table goes to die; that's what Craigslist is for, buddy. Lose the threadbare recliner and put your collection of baseball caps or hockey jerseys in storage. Call me crazy, but clothing is meant to be put on the body, not hung on a wall.

I hate to break it to you, but you're not a caveman. You're a guy who hasn't shaved in three days. Wash off your Pleistocene funk, turn on the light, and for God's sake, stop grunting. If not, I'll have no choice but to whack you with a woolly mammoth bone, which is going to leave a mark, no matter how you try to cover it up with your loincloth.

MERCURY IN RETROGRADE

PUNCH RATING

I've been dreading this day for awhile. By most accounts, god-damned Mercury is going into retrograde again. What this means is that Mercury appears to us earthlings to slow down and move backwards for several weeks.

It also means that I'm fucked.

I am often suspicious of anything with a whiff of woo-woo, but over the years, I've learned to heed the power of this punk-ass planet. Emails go missing, interpersonal communication goes down the crapper, misunderstandings abound, business deals fall through, my motherfucking motherboard dies. It's around this time that I turn to the bottle.

How this little bitch planet wields so much impish power is beyond me, as well as people a whole lot higher than me on the intellectual food chain. The one thing I do know is that this ass-illogical shit has gots to stop. I

> **FACT OF THE MATTER**
> ✦ In Roman mythology, Mercury is the messenger of the gods, and for some reason the planet seems to wreak havoc on communication and relationships when it's in retrograde.

think a call to NASA is in order. Maybe if we can hit it hard enough with a monster missile, we can change its orbit and stop the insanity.

But until we make that happen, back your files up…seriously.

MIMES

Well, if you insist.

These blanc buffoons place themselves in my line of ire the minute they rock the whiteface. Dammit to hell, Marcel Marceau! What have you wrought?

Riddle me curious, but what compels a kookaloo (in French, *kookalou*) to tumble down the rabbit hole and sign up for a mime class? Did he have a grandparent who always seemed to have trouble with his invisible umbrella on windy days? Did she see a Doug Henning television special in the '70s that made her hot for French sailor shirts? Does he think miming will lend him a certain *je ne sais quoi*? I do know what: *Il est stupide*.

Mimes need to be rounded up and herded into a box in front of the Centre Pompidou. Tag these douchebaguettes with a black-and-white computer chip. And if anyone tries to escape the box, imaginary or otherwise, I'm going to throw back a *pain au chocolat* before going *un peu* Marquis de Sade on the rogue clown by

> **FACT OF THE MATTER**
> ✤ The English predecessor to the mime was the mummer, or should I say dumber?

choking him with his fey neckerchief. There won't be a need to draw a sad clown teardrop near his right eye. Those tears will be real, *mon ami*.

Clowns may be creepy, but mimes are the fiends who moonwalk through my nightmares.

MIRRORLESS DRESSING ROOMS

PUNCH RATING

Mirror, mirror, on the wall, should I buy this dress? What's your call?

Cricket. Cricket.

There's no mirror in sight, not even of the fat or funhouse variety. Are you trying to be merciful, preventing me from seeing a fashion misstep? Nay, I think you have something more insidious in mind.

Here I am, stuck in this crawlspace of a dressing room, shimmying into some garment. If I miraculously manage to zip, hook, and button everything, I'd actually like to see how I look in it. But if I slink out to the communal mirror to eyeball the damage, sycophantic sales associates slither up, doing their best to convince me that sausage casing is the new black.

Yeah, no.

To be fair, there might be other reasons you tricked out your store with closets instead of dressing rooms. You might have broken your last mirror and are only two years into your seven years of bad luck. Maybe you're Medusa and want to make sure no one has a reflective surface when you're trying to turn them to stone. Or you might just be cheap.

But I think the most likely reason that the mirror has no place is that you're trying to be wily, flushing me out of the retail brush so you can get me in your sights and kill me with false compliments.

It's time to fight back. I think I should call upon the evil queen from *Snow White*, who knows a thing or two about the power of reflection. She can turn you into a wizened old witch in a bad dress and hair desperately in need of conditioner. Reflect on that.

MIXOLOGISTS

PUNCH RATING

I recently went to a new watering hole, all warm, low lighting and fancy bar menu designed by someone with interesting eyewear. The drinks, with the clever names you'd expect from a hipster bar that requires a secret handshake to enter, were made out of exotic ingredients. My pal and I were parched, so we just ordered up two Tanqueray and tonics.

No Tanqueray. No problem. I can roll with a locally distilled and handcrafted gin.

Minutes ticked by. The thirst mounted.

Finally, our waitress appeared with a pair of ginger-colored cocktails gleaming in their old-fashioned glasses. "Good news! We have this amazing tonic; it's made from Peruvian tree bark."

My face became the visual version of a needle scratching a record. Peruvian tree bark in my gin and tonic. That explained the tea-stained color.

Again, I'd like to think I'm open-minded. But hell if it didn't taste vaguely like cinnamon-laced apple. And it was as flat as Keira Knightley's chest. Needless to say, I sent that drink back to South America and gave my best stinkeye to the bartender. Excuse me, *mixologist.*

Handcrafted bitters infused with rare herbs. Schnapps produced in a tiny Alpine hamlet only during avalanche season. Drink names that combine the mixologist's last vacation destination with a weather phenomenon or natural disaster. No, I do not want a Cabo San Tsunami, Amsterdammit! What's next? Vodka made from Brussels sprouts?

Mixologists are easy to spot. Their plumage comes in the form of a natty vest, and they all vaguely resemble Joseph Gordon-Levitt.

They have an extensive knowledge of absinthe and the ruined men who loved her, are judgmental of anyone else's cocktail-making abilities, and rejoice in taking half an hour to make a Ramos gin fizz (which, admittedly, is delicious).

They pride themselves on being an exhaustive repository on all things boozy. If you want

the back story on that fifteen-year-old Calvados, the mixologist is your man. But if you want a gin and tonic without a side of "I know better—let me make you a new and improved cocktail," head to your closest dive bar. You can get pissed drunk instead of pissed off.

MOLLY RINGWALD'S PROM DRESS IN PRETTY IN PINK

PUNCH RATING 👊 👊 👊 👊 👊

Biggest. Cinematic. Letdown. Ever.

After showing mad personal style throughout the entire movie (no one, and I mean no one, rocks pearls and flowered fabric like Molly Ringwald), the girl shows up defiantly at prom to prove to the world and to Blaine, the insipid boy with the crazy eyes and white pleated pants, that she's not broken.

Um, it's just a thought, but she might have chosen a more suitable dress to take a stand in, something that didn't scream "home-sewn hot mess."

Andie should have left Fiona's dress alone. I want to bitch slap that polyester Frankenfrock with the collar and mesh insert, shred it, and burn it. Oh, wait—it's probably treated with flame retardant. Fire bad.

Let's hope Andie got that scholarship and used it at FIT or Parsons.

> **FACT OF THE MATTER**
> ✦ Costume designer Marilyn Vance worked on some of my all-time favorite movies, including *Die Hard, Road House, The Untouchables, Pretty Woman,* and *The Breakfast Club,* which makes her apromination almost forgivable. Almost.

MOTEL ART

PUNCH RATING

When visiting Fallingwater a few years back, a guide told us that Frank Lloyd Wright designed low ceilings and lots of windows into the famous home so people would be encouraged to go outside.

Well, motel art is about as far away as you can get from FLW, but the result is the same. I want to flee the premises when I am in a motel room dripping with bad art.

But first, I go into the bathroom to see if my eyes are bleeding.

Thomas Kinkade–like landscapes, art that is reminiscent of the cover of Duran Duran's "Rio," prints of ships and sandpipers, still lifes that match the bedspread—it's all one stinky art fart. Motel rooms are where art goes to die a slow, faded, badly framed death.

Next time, don't take an Ambien to get to sleep. Take down the art, turn it around, and stick it in the closet next to the ironing board. You'll sleep like a baby.

MR. DARCY

PUNCH RATING

Over the years, I've been sucked in again and again by your sang-froid, your stateliness, your brooding tall, dark, and handsomeness, and your ability to make me hot just by climbing out of your pond, soaking wet and fully clothed.

Since you are, well, not real, I've looked from here to Hampshire for a flesh-and-blood Fitzwilliam. I have not fared well. I entertained one yahoo because I thought he'd look dashing astride a horse wearing one of those long coats you fancy. I swoon at the thought of those things, the way they sweep the ground as you walk with determination, legs encased in breeches and knee boots....

I digress.

I dated another gentleman who, like you, was sensitive and felt deeply. But he didn't act on shit. He just stewed in his emo juices. Miserly compliments and infrequent attentions kept me wondering about his intentions until he laissez-faired us to death. I mean, how long is a girl supposed to hang in there, in hopes of securing moody blues like you?

Let's not forget the know-it-all narcissist who had clearly spent some time at Pemberley in your company. He was a real treat, spamming familiars and strangers with his prideful advice and prejudiced judgment. Proclamations as pillow talk don't exactly blow my petticoat up, sir.

Darcy, you're a prick. You don't like to dance. You throw your best friend around like a ventriloquist's dummy, telling him what to do and say. Bingley's one step away from sitting on your lap. Not cool. You publicly skewer a gal for her lack of connections and lowly parentage—we can't get enough of that—while secretly admiring her moxie and form. You bottle up your feelings until they bubble over and you blurt out your affections, telling her you love her despite your better judgment. Be still, my heart. This is going to catch a lady off guard, particularly since she's spent nigh on a year avoiding you, wondering what she ever did to irk your shit, and thinking you're a grade-A, navel-gazing jackwipe.

Yeah, you came through in the end, saving the Bennet family from social disgrace and all that. Always the hero, Mr.

> **FACT OF THE MATTER**
> ◆ Get this: A sex pheromone in male mouse urine (you didn't expect that, did you?) was named Darcin in honor of Mr. Darcy. Sort of takes the piss out of my punch, doesn't it?

Darcy, you've ruined me for the real world of dating. No man can measure up and yet, I don't want to hold them to your standard, since you—how can I put this delicately?—suck.

You've screwed me, and, indeed sir, not in a good way.

NAIL ART

PUNCH RATING 👊 👊

I've slowly but surely turned into a fuddy-duddy, a finger-wagger of the first degree. I don't like exposed bra straps and still believe in slips. I think hair colors not found in nature are stupid (I'm looking at you, Nicole Richie and Kelly Osbourne). And I find nail art to be like nails on my beauty chalkboard.

I prefer short nails in one color, often Black Onyx or Russian Navy. I don't like talons that have been whittled down to the point where they could pick a lock. And I certainly don't like nails with crazy designs and different colors. For starters, fingernail designs and colors often skew trashy, like Hello Kitty just got hired at the Bunny Ranch, or Tara Reid, well, just Tara Reid. Plus, nail art is anything but cheap, unless you're using the press-on variety. Nail polish chips so fast. Getting your favorite team's logo on your fingertips seems like an awfully expensive venture for such a short lifespan. And if you're doing it at home, it invariably looks sloppy, unless you're ambidextrous and detail-obsessed. You start out with the best of intentions and bottles of pink, green, and yellow polish and wind up looking like a crazy colorblind person wearing a botched craft project.

> **FACT OF THE MATTER**
> ✦ E! rolled out the "mani-cam" on the red carpet to showcase actresses' manicures and nail art. We rolled our eyes. Elizabeth Moss gave it the finger, while Julianne Moore, Reese Witherspoon, and Jennifer Aniston just flat-out refused to do it.

But the biggest reason that I turn away from these manic-cures is that they pull focus. I want people to look at me, not my fingernails. I'm not a vehicle for miniature portraits, landscapes, and abstracts; I am the work of art. My manicure doesn't make me interesting; it just makes me polished.

NAKED PREGNANCY PORTRAITS

PUNCH RATING

You're gorgeous and juicy, ladyfriend, but you're not Demi Moore. I don't want to see you naked when you're not pregnant. I sure as shit don't want to see you drop trou with a bun in the oven.

I don't have a problem with you hiring Annie Leibovitz to capture this oh-so-important period in your life. Just don't ask me to pore over the album, attend the portrait unveiling, or suffer your new two-for-one Facebook photo.

Treacly pregnancy photos bring navel gazing to a new level. Literally. In fact, your new outie is all you can see. Don't get me wrong: I can't wait to see the new addition to your family. In the meantime, just show me the sonogram.

> **FACT OF THE MATTER**
> ✦ Demi Moore stars in the mother of all pregnancy portraits, snapped by Annie Leibovitz in 1991 for the cover of *Vanity Fair*.

NAMASTE

When I hear someone say "namaste," I want to beat them and their sustainable clothing with a rain stick. I mean, fine, say it at the end of yoga class…if you absolutely have to. But when I hear it outside of the ashram, it harshes my mellow. The likely culprits are people who get their kids hopped up on carob chips and let them run around Trader Joe's because they are "spirited."

Namaste means "The light in me honors the light in you." When I'm in shavasana (during my rare forays into yoga) and I hear this, I throw up a little in my mouth. Laying on my back, well, you can imagine that this isn't a good thing. The light in me wants to knock your lights out or, better yet, reach in and rip out your heart chakra. Saying "namaste" doesn't make you enlightened, it just makes you a tool in an organic bamboo hoodie.

> **FACTS OF THE MATTER**
> + Like "aloha," namaste is both a greeting and farewell in India.
> + The pressed-palms namaste bow appeared 4,000 years ago on clay seals, just proving that a lot of generations have escaped my wrath through the peace that comes with death.

NEW YEAR'S EVE

PUNCH RATING 👊 👊 👊 👊 👊

New Year's Eve is always memorable. To wit:

1970-SOMETHING: Mom and Dad went to some party at the Holiday Inn and left me at home with my two older brothers. My Mrs. Beasley doll was decapitated that night, a harbinger of the tragic NYEs that were to come.

1989: I was freshly heartbroken and covering the Rose Bowl for the Michigan yearbook, so I was in L.A. with the staff photographer. We wound up at a giant alumni NYE party in the Valley, where I ran into my ex-boyfriend with his new girlfriend. I spent the night walking around the party with a twelve-pack, dispensing beers to people who had a reason to live. I then sped back to the hotel on one of the freeways in a fugue state, stayed up all night, and then downed gallons of black coffee in the Rose Bowl press box…where I was seated next to my ex, a sports editor for the university newspaper. Oh, and Michigan lost that year.

1990: This year found me in Detroit, partying it up with my college friends at a shindig at the top of the RenCen. I wish I could say I was drunk. I went up a down escalator…or tried to. After a scary ambulance ride to Detroit Receiving with a driver who resembled Large Marge, I spent five hours getting my Frankenknee stitched up while surrounded by an urban version of Hieronymus Bosch's "Garden of Earthly Delights." I couldn't bend my knee for two weeks.

2003: Fast forward a decade and change, and you'd find me at Bob & Barbara's, a dope dive bar in Philly, watching my boyfriend kiss a guy in front of me. I walked out and left him behind. I wish I had the sense to ditch New Year's Eve as well.

> **FACT OF THE MATTER**
> ✦ We have the Scots to thank for more than kilts; "Auld Lang Syne" is a Scots poem by Robert Burns set to a traditional folk song. Tartan-colored crap.

2004: Got stoned with my best friend while teaching her to knit and watching *Gigli*. This officially marked my march into spinsterdom.

2008: Me, a sorta boyfriend (who drank too much and eventually passed out), and two gay bears sat on the couch and watched *Mythbusters*. Holla. Oh yeah, he broke things off the next week via IM. This really set the tone for the massive suck that was 2009.

In short, New Year's Eve should be forgotten and never brought to mind.

NEW YORKER CARTOONS

PUNCH RATING

I have never, ever subscribed to *The New Yorker*.

There. I said it.

Call me unsophisticated, a troglodyte, a knob, whatev. I'm okay with it. I read *The Pew Yorker* occasionally when hanging out with friends more refined than me. But after eyeballing an issue, I walk away. It makes me feel stupid, and I'm already full up in that department.

It's not the articles. I can deal with a lengthy piece now and again, and I'm always able to soldier through "Shouts & Murmurs" and reviews with little damage to my ego.

And it's not the pompous Mr. Peanut dandy who represents. I get it. Dudes with monocles read *The New Yorker*. As they should. It's their thing, along with spats and a penchant for crème brûlée (not to mention words using the accent aigu).

It's the goddamn cartoons. When I'm in a dentist's office, I'd still rather reach for *Highlights* than *The New Yorker*. I can always detect what doesn't belong in a picture but fuck if I know what is clever or funny about a cartoon of a dude who, while rak-

> **FACT OF THE MATTER**
>
> ◆ *The New Yorker* and its cartoons have been confounding folks since the magazine's inception in 1925. The most reprinted cartoon is Peter Steiner's 1993 drawing of two dogs in a front of a computer with the caption, "On the Internet, nobody knows you're a dog." That, I get.

ing leaves, holds up a maple leaf and says to his wife, "They're all pretty, but this one is my favorite." Am I missing something? Like IQ points or my frontal lobe? I'd like to change this caption to read: "You know, this could be dipped in resin or metal to make a five-pointed weapon to kill me with." That I would understand. That I could get behind.

NON-PRESCRIPTION EYEGLASSES

PUNCH RATING

Guess what? I'm selfish.

I'm also blind as a bat. I've worn -12.5 Coke bottles over my eyes since second grade. It makes me blind with rage when I see hipsters trying to look emo, ironic, brainy, sexy librarianish, or Weezery by donning a pair of frames.

If you don't need them as your third and fourth eyes, if your peepers don't look like tiny blinking specks or giant dilated saucers behind your lenses, back away from the Oliver Peoples and pass by Pearl Vision.

Buy a hat or get a tattoo, and let me have this.

> **FACT OF THE MATTER**
> ✦ I once had a date ask me to take off my glasses to see if my eyes were really that small. No, jackass. It's just that my prescription is -12.5...like your IQ.

OBLIGATORY STANDING OVATIONS

PUNCH RATING

SCENE: A local theater troupe is gamely putting on a show, despite a terrible script, missed cues, unrecoverable gaffes, and wooden Keanu-worthy acting. The curtain falls, and the players breathe a collective sigh of relief. They can flee to the darkness of the wings.

And then the curtain rises for a final bow. The actors see the audience clapping enthusiastically and, miraculously, rising out of their seats. They wonder to themselves, "Were they watching the same play we just performed?" And... scene.

Nope, these actors aren't in an artsy-fartsy *Twilight Zone*. They're simply living in the era of the obligatory standing ovation. Standing Os are given out these days as easily as Kanye West's opinion. They're the adult ver-

> **FACT OF THE MATTER**
>
> ❖ A standing ovation wasn't always the ultimate accolade. In ancient Rome, returning military commanders whose battles didn't quite rate "triumph" status were celebrated with a "close but no cigar" ovation, a word that comes from the Latin *ovo*, "I rejoice."

sion of the "everybody gets a trophy" culture. Whether it's a concert by an ancient band on their fifth farewell tour, a hack comic with hackneyed bits, or a homegrown production, audiences can't stop themselves from simpering all over the performers—even if the show was a steaming pile of *merde*. Standing only encourages their delusion-fueled performance.

When the curtain goes up, stand down, for the love of God, country, and good taste. Send a different kind of message with your anemic applause: Get thee to rehearsal. Keep workshopping your shit. Take an acting class. *Practice.* Raise your standards, not your body.

PAJAMAS AS OUTERWEAR

PUNCH RATING 👊 👊 👊 👊 👊

While I'd like to think of life as one big pillow fight, it's not. It's not a slumber party, and the frozen food section is not Maria Greene's basement, as much as I sometimes wish it were. So why are you wearing pajamas and slippers as you're reaching for those Totino's Pizza Rolls? Put them back and put some clothes on. I think you can find some in Aisle 10.

Dressing has become more and more casual as we slip on flip flops and pull on fleece hoodies for all sorts of occasions. But nightgowns, flannel PJs, and bathrobes cross the Casual Friday line and step into the territory of the crazy, depressed, or those coping with any other state of mind that might demand medication or, at the very least, light therapy.

Admit it: You've thrown in the towel. You might as well just curl up in the fetal position under a Snuggie and give up. I won't kick you while you're down, but do me a favor and keep your crazy behind closed

> **FACT OF THE MATTER**
> ✦ If you need any sort of cautionary tale about the slippery slope of wearing pajamas outside the house, you only need to look at peopleofwalmart.com.

(perhaps locked) doors. If you don't, I'm going to surprise you in the bedding aisle and whack you with a big-ass pillow until you wake the fuck up and change out of your crib clothes.

PARENTS WHO GIVE THEIR OFFSPRING NAMES STARTING WITH THE SAME INITIAL

PUNCH RATING

FACT OF THE MATTER

→ These days, the most popular first letter for boys' names is J; for girls' names, it's A. Expectant parents: Back away from the Jacobs and the Avas, please.

Forget the Octo-Mom; I'm way more disturbed by *19 Kids & Counting*, the TLC show about the Duggar family. Yeah, there are nineteen of them. I could comment about the crazy number of children, but that would be like shooting fish in a barrel. That's not what gripes my ass. Rather, it irritates me when parents give all their kids names starting with the same initial. Jordyn, Jason, Jinger, Jessa, Jill, Joshua, John-David, Jennifer, Jackson, Justin, James— enough already! Would it hurt you to throw a Kevin or Stacey in there, John Jacob Jingleheimer Jackass?

The Duggars aren't alone. I grew up surrounded by kids who came from alliterative households. Carol was kin to Cathy and Christine; Dan's siblings were Dave, Debbie, and Diana. Dumb.

I don't even know where to begin with George Foreman.

(For the record, my brothers are Chris and John, and my step-sibs are Jay, Joe, Paul, Amy, Denise, and Annette, because, obviously, my parents rock.)

PARKING HOGS

You know them. Chances are, you also want to punch these selfish fucks in the face (or shatter their windshields with that baseball bat you keep in the trunk for "emergencies"). I'm talking about the asscaps who park their precious car/truck/SUV/crotch rocket/shitbox caboose over several parking spots. I suspect they want to avoid any damage from neighboring car doors. I got news for you and your insurance provider: Splaying your vehicle across several spots is only going to draw attention to it, and not in any kind of good way.

I have the same violent feelings about this parking violation as I do about people who hate to park their car on the street instead of a garage, or are scared to drive it into the big bad city. If you are that worried about your ride, you prolly shouldn't take it out of the cul de sac.

But maybe you have a good reason for flunking your driving test on a daily basis. Perhaps you're visually challenged. Or confused—no, that line in front of you is not a guide for centering your Hummer.

Get your OCD on and make it a challenge NOT to touch either line, instead of straddling it like Tara Reid on a mechanical bull. If you keep it up, I'm going to get jiggy with the parking piggy. I'm going to drive up your insurance premiums when I smash into your beloved Beemer from whatever angle you've provided me with. And if that doesn't do the trick, I'm going to really go Kathy Bates on you and get out the sledgehammer. I'll make sure you're not driving or parking anything but a wheelchair anytime soon.

> **FACT OF THE MATTER**
> ✦ Parking spots are generally seven and a half to nine feet wide. When you have a ginormous SUV muffin topping into my space, it's no surprise that I'm going to ding your paint job with my door.

PASSWORDS

PUNCH RATING

Every since I was a wittle gurl, I liked security. In the form of my binkie, my mother's bedtime kiss, a sturdy deadbolt. And I thought passwords were the shit. They were currency into the cool kids' clubhouse, sometimes literally.

> **FACT OF THE MATTER**
> ✦ Believe it or not, passwords predate the internet. In ancient times, sentries would make people supply a password, also called a watchword, and would let them pass if they answered correctly.

And then…the internet. In its infancy, I could use one password—a pet's name, some iteration of my birth date, a word that always makes me giggle—for everything.

And then…now. With secure office servers, viruses, hackers, the cloud, and just plain annoyingly efficient websites requiring frequent password resets, my mind and my secret codes are a jumble. Some are written down in various notebooks, some are trapped in my mind, hanging out on the trash heap of other lost memories like the last name of that boyfriend who always kept his gum tucked behind a molar when kissing me, and some are plopped God knows where on my laptop.

Technology is supposed to make life easier, not remind me at every turn of how old and infirm my mind is becoming.

TIWTPITF2012 – TruLove99 – Haircut100 – Butterfield8 – LakersRule86 – IH8Scrabble – maisoui123 – FUpassword

No, they're not vanity plates. These are my pathetic attempts to find the right combination to unlock my iTunes/Facebook/Twitter/Pinterest/LinkedIn/Outlook/GoogleYouTubeFlickr/bank/investment/mobile provider/online retailer account. Maybe I should just reset everything right now to Amnesiac4ever.

And don't talk to me about security questions.

PATCHOULI

PUNCH RATING 👊 👊 👊 👊 👊

Damn you, patchouli! I cannot stomach your musky stink one minute longer. Much like peach schnapps, a whiff of you makes me throw up a little in my mouth. While this isn't a good thing in any situation, it's especially bad in this case, since I really need to breathe through my mouth to avoid you.

On a recent flight, I sat next to a couple of old-school hippies. They were ripe. I aimed the vent right at my nose and tried my best to sleep. But my puny

> **FACT OF THE MATTER**
> ✦ In addition to repelling people, patchouli has been used as an insect repellent and even as an antidote to snakebites.

olfactory sense was no match for their mighty stench.

What's worse, if I brush against anything with you on it, your funk spams itself all over me and I can't get it off. Can you imagine my nausea-laced mortification when I bumped into someone while doused in patchouli right before an important meeting? I was trying to impress, and I smelled like Haight-Ashbury during a 1969 heat wave.

To those fans of ratchouli, let me just say that dabbing on an overpowering fragrance in lieu of bathing only works for the French. Are you trying to brand yourself as a free spirit? Newsflash, Sunshine Rainbow Quinoa, you're trying to fit in by wearing comfort sandals and reeking of patchoupee, just as much as if you were wearing the latest trend and spritzing yourself with a designer fragrance.

I think a Silkwood-style scrubdown is in order to exfoliate that shit down the drain, followed by a tomato juice bath to neutralize any lingering skunk. Finally, my daisy-fresh friends and I will form a circle around you and pummel you with hacky sacks, while alternately spraying aerosol deodorant and Febreeze in your general direction.

PAYPAL

PUNCH RATING

If it ain't broke, don't fix it.

That adage works for things like your favorite lasagna recipe, but does it really work for a transactional site like PayPal? I want their engineers to be constantly upgrading security and improving their interface so

they're never put in a position to fix anything. I will admit that PayPal did finally—after years with a crappy site that looked like it was made for $500 by a self-taught "designer"—retool the site. So there's that.

However.

As a seller, it's still a pain in the ass to navigate your way to saved "Buy" buttons or to create new buttons for your products. For this service, PayPal takes three percent for every online payment. I saw *Office Space;* those pennies add up every time PayPal transfers money from someone's bank to yours. But the real reason to punch PayPal is, as a buyer, I could be providing my detailed financial information to a hacker in a remote North Korean village. Also, like He-Man, PayPal has the power, which it can wield indiscriminately, locking accounts for no reason and providing terrible to nonexistent customer service.

Do I really want to PayPal to play, trusting my checking account or credit card info to the likes of this service, the Comcast of online payment systems? No, so computer engineers and tech entrepreneurs, please put your considerable IQ and VC together and create a better alternative, so I can finally start that Etsy store that's the cornerstone of my longterm retirement plan.

PEACH SCHNAPPS

PUNCH RATING

Setting: Triangle Fraternity, somewhere in Michigan, sometime in the '80s…

Enter a brainy coed wearing a peach-colored shirt from Contempo Casuals and that awesome pair of Guess jeans with the zippers at the ankles. You know what I'm talking about.

Well, the brainiac wasn't so smart that particular night, as she

> **FACT OF THE MATTER**
> ✦ German schnapps is clear with a light fruit flavor. Peach schnapps is something else. An Amercian creation, it is a blend of grain spirits, fruit flavor, sugar, and glycerin, which in combination brings to mind cough syrup.

was also packing a pint of peach schnapps. Even though the engineering fraternity usually had an open bar at its parties, it was inconvenient to interrupt a heated game of eight-ball or Twister to get a fresh Fuzzy Navel. So she brought her own, alternately taking swigs and reapplying her frosty Clinique lipstick, the one she got as a gift with purchase.

You know what happened next.

Wildly drunk, she had the walking spins, bent down to pick up something, accidentally got kneed in the eye, yacked, and finally passed out after Maria or someone got her back to South Quad.

The next day was not pretty, and not only because of her black eye.

To this day, the less-than-brainy graduate can suss out that treacly syrup in any punch. Just a soupçon of that smell brings on da acid reflux. To add insult to my injury, it doesn't smell or taste remotely like the real thing. Peach schnapps gives peaches a bad rap. It's time to punch the evil that is peach schnapps in the schnoz. Better yet, I'm going to pour it into a vat near Fraternity Row, set it on fire, and let coeds get that warm, fuzzy feeling without the threat of puking.

PENIS NAMES

PUNCH RATING

Big Daddy, Cock Hudson, Unihorn, Richard Dixon, Carl, One-Eyed Willie, Casanova, Sir Lancelot, Ralph.

You see where I'm going with this. If you're a dude, chances are good that you've dubbed your dick.

Ever since I read *Forever...* by Judy Blume in junior high, I've been aware that guys have a penchant for naming their junk. I can appreciate the package as much as the next girl. I just don't need to be on a first-name basis with it.

I've got a few names for your Johnson, Junior, and none of them are found in the Big Book of Baby Names. Your little Richard doesn't have a birth certifi-

cate, it doesn't have a separate heartbeat, and it doesn't merit a name. While my lady bits are remarkable, I'm not christening them and requesting a Social Security number. They are much loved, yet remain nameless.

Your constant cumpanion needs to be put in its place, namely your drawers. And I know just the thing to turn Voldemort's Wand into He Who Shall Not Be Named.

Say hello to my little friend. Its name is Left Fist and it's ready to, uh, whack these upstarts into global amnesia anonymity. A penis by any other name would sound as beat.

PEOPLE WHO BLAB ON RED-EYES

PUNCH RATING 👊 👊

You've made your connection, and he's in the aisle seat. It's like some sort of dreamy Sofia Coppola movie, and you're the romantic lead. You're enjoying pillow talk with a sexy stranger who may be your true love, or at least your ticket into the Mile High Club. Sorry to interrupt, but can you do me a favor?

Shut. The. Fuck. UP.

I don't care what time zone we are currently flying over—my internal clock and my wristwatch say it's 3:30 in the morning. I took this flight and an Ambien because I'm good at sleeping on planes. I have my rituals: I don't drink caffeine, I listen to Joni Mitchell laced with Sufjan Stevens, and I wrap myself in my giant knitted shawl.

All I ask is that a bratty toddler not kick my seat and that you Shut. The. Fuck. UP.

Even with headphones on, I can hear you yammering away with your life story and relationship history (which, from the sounds of it, you might want to keep to yourself until the third date; just a thought).

When I ask if you could lower

> **FACT OF THE MATTER**
> ✦ In the 2005 film *Red Eye*, poor Rachel McAdams makes the mistake of talking with a sexy stranger, who turns out to be a terrorist planning an assassination. Moral of the story: Never talk on a red-eye.

your voice because every other single person on the plane is trying to sleep (as evidenced by the pitch-black cabin and profusion of navy blankets, sleep masks, and earbuds), you stare at me as if I just killed your dog. I explain that of course you have the right to talk, but that I'm just asking for some courtesy toward your fellow travelers. Bring the volume down or I'm going to descend into madness and punch you in the face. Forget about true love's kiss from Prince Charming in 18C. Your kiss is on my fist when they turn out the lights.

PEOPLE WHO DON'T BELIEVE IN TV

PUNCH RATING

I've been on loads of first dates that proved to be the last date as well. None of these guys were sociopaths or suffering from acute halitosis. Oh sure, some were inconsiderate and some were cheap, but none of them were bad guys per se (the bad boys usually get a second date).

No, my biggest beef with many of my dates was that they didn't own a television.

> **FACT OF THE MATTER**
> ❖ In his book, *Everything Bad Is Good for You,* Stephen Johnson makes the case for watching TV. When it comes to television, even a turd of a reality show, Johnson argues that it's not the content that matters, but the cognitive work your mind is doing while staring at Snooki's cooch.

They weren't moving cross-country or suffering from a broken cathode ray tube. It may seem inconceivable, but there are folks in the world who don't believe in TV.

Bend over and take a deep breath. It helps the dizziness.

I watch more than my share of TV. *America's Next Top Model* is not for everyone, I grant you. But for me, being on the pop culture superhighway is part of what defines me, as well as what educates and entertains me. Watching TV provides me with conversational currency. What in the world do these pretentious fucks have to talk about? Seriously?

Without a TV, flat-screen or otherwise, how can you stay apprised of Tyra's latest tutorials? Or get unexpectedly sucked into a Ken Burns documentary or Shark Week? Or bear witness to the majesty of a royal wedding or the maid of honor's ass?

You can't.

I'm not talking about the high-tech nerd who streams stuff on his laptop or catches the latest episode of *Dr. Who* on an iPhone. No, he's exempt from my rage. He isn't throwing the baby out with the RGB bathwater. I'm talking about the cappuccino intellectual who stuffs a tattered copy of Proust into an NPR tote bag while listening to Philip Glass and sporting a fedora.

In other words, a massive tool.

PEOPLE WHO STOP AT THE TOP OF ESCALATORS

PUNCH RATING

Um, excuse me. You there at the top of the escalator. No, not you. That guy. The completely unaware yambag checking his watch, looking at a map, looking anywhere but behind him. EXCUSE ME! I'm about to rear-end you, and not in a good way. Where the fuck do you think I and the rest of moving humanity queued up behind you are going to go?

Up your ass, that's where. Escalators don't break for boobs,

> **FACT OF THE MATTER**
> ✦ The first working escalator was built alongside a pier at Coney Island in 1896. You'd think people would have learned how to use them by now.

Einstein, and neither does my ire. I'm going to create my own moving walkway and I'm going to call it "Your Back." Are you listening now?

PEOPLE WHO WATCH ALL THE MOVIE CREDITS

PUNCH RATING

The movie's over. I know this because I hear the strains of some treacly Adina Menzel power ballad and I see credits rolling.

This is my cue to vamanos.

There's just one problem. Peen Shalit next to me is gazing at the screen as though it's the beginning of *Star Wars*.

Excuse me, sir, did you work on the film? Are you in the business? Did you happen to be in Utah for Sundance last year? Is Zach Galifianakis your second cousin? Do you sleep with your eyes open?

No? Then why are you still sitting there? You're blocking my passage, and the ushers need to clean up the remnants of your jumbo combo snack box before the next screening.

Sure, if outtakes or additional footage are part of the credits,

> **FACT OF THE MATTER**
> ✦ The closing credits for the extended edition of *The Lord of the Rings: The Return of the King* clocks in at just under ten minutes, ample time to claw off your own face.

I'm right there with you. I don't want to miss Will Ferrell's ad-libbing hilarity either. But that's not usually the case. If you have to watch the credits because you're avoiding going home to an empty or angry house or because you're an aficionado who says "film" instead of "movie" and takes your two-week vacation during your city's film festival, at least have the decency to sit in the middle of a row so I don't have to play impromptu aisle Twister. Consider doing what any self-respecting film buff does: study IMDB when you get home.

If I have to give you one more lap dance as I'm exiting stage right, I'm going to pack a boom mic in my bag along with my contraband snacks and go Darth Maul on you.

POLAR BEAR PLUNGES

PUNCH RATING 👊 👊 👊

I love the water. I hate the cold. But in the Rochambeau of my preferences, cold trumps water by a nautical mile, because I can't wrap my mind around polar bear clubs, those collections of brave souls who drop trou and run into the water to celebrate New Year's Day or some such bullshit holiday. Dudes, that's what drinking champagne and bungling the lyrics to "Auld Lang Syne" is for.

I can't bring myself to jump in and out of a plunge pool after a sauna or hot tub. I can only walk into an alpine lake up to my ankles, no matter how sweaty the hike that preceded it. And it takes me a long while to ease into the ocean, even if it's Florida in August. A polar bear swim is not on this girl's bucket list.

If the folly of diving into icy waters isn't sufficiently crazytown (isn't the Titanic's survival rate cautionary tale enough?), we also have the *naked* polar bear plunges. I don't want to see that when you're warm and erect. I certainly don't want to see your shriveled twigs and berries.

I can do lots of things that are good for my health but that don't require the bracing winter waters of a northern lake, sea, or ocean: nutritional sup-

> **FACT OF THE MATTER**
> ✤ Vancouver's Polar Bear Swim Club has been active since 1920; upward of 2,000 hardy souls annually take the plunge on New Year's Day. Without college bowl games, I guess Canadians don't have anything better to do.

plements, Pilates, kale salad, cardio. There's only one way I'm going to experience an icy liquid: in a rocks glass.

POLLEN

I know plants need you to grow and shit, but do you have to rub it in our faces (especially my right eye, which is almost swollen shut because of your need to be front and center)? I swear, you're just like Kanye: If

FACT OF THE MATTER
✦ Ragweed is the biggest offender of hay fever, which affects ten to twenty percent of Americans. And that's nothing to sniff at.

we stop talking about you for a second, you whip up a new controversy to get carried along in the wind. Get over yourself and let something else shine for once. Have you ever considered that mold spores might like a moment now and again?

I don't mean to be a major ragweed, but enough is enough. I'm tired—seriously, I need a nap—of breathing only through my mouth. It's time to make hay, not hay fever, while the sun shines, which means I need to wash you and your allergen pals outta my hair, off of my skin, and down the drain. I'm going to drown your greedy sinus-squatting ass in vats of antihistimines and decongestants. Maybe that'll teach you to keep to your turf and fertilize flora, not my nasal passages…microscopic bitch.

PRECIOUS MOMENTS

PUNCH RATING

These china clowns, cherubs, and rascals skipped through the nightmares of my youth, and I'm still holding a grudge (when I'm not huddled in the fetal position). They traveled in big-eyed packs, alongside Love's Baby Soft, window crystals, and rainbow stickers. They may have been pastel, but they were far from soothing.

Precious Moments really exploded when I was knee-sock-deep into Catholic school, so it was no surprise that I was initially drawn to their cheeky innocence. I had one particularly adorbs lamb that I lifted from a nativity scene. I wanted to hug it and kiss it and call it my own. After about five minutes, however, I moved onto Shaun Cassidy and put my porcelain pet out to pasture.

But that was not enough to corral the horror. Tears of a clown would rain down my face at the thought of the baby mimes and toddler princesses littering the Hallmark store at the local strip mall. What really gets my goat now is the thought of all these evil Enesco eyesores sitting on shelves and in cabinets around the world. I'll finally give them an actual reason for those sad eyes: my hammer coming toward their shiny, happy faces.

> **FACT OF THE MATTER**
> ✦ For fans wanting to make a pilgrimage, the Precious Moments Chapel can be found in all its wide-eyed glory in Carthage, Missouri.

PROLIFIC DEAD PEOPLE

PUNCH RATING 👊 👊 👊 👊

I see dead people…everywhere.

As if I didn't already have enough self-loathing, dead people are churning out more stuff than I am. Tupac seems to have a new album of unreleased tracks dropping every other year. Michael Jackson had barely settled into his cryogenic chamber before the output kicked in. Jeff Buckley and Stieg Larsson didn't cash in until they checked out. Like another day at the office, the late David Foster Wallace posthumously published another book that none of us will be smart enough

> **FACT OF THE MATTER**
> ◆ Tupac Shakur has released seven posthumous studio albums. This does not include the live (ironic, *n'est pas*?), compilation, remix, and soundtrack albums, not to mention his recent "live" performance at Coachella.

to understand. In a creepy turn of events, Nat King Cole duetted with his daughter Natalie from beyond the grave, even managing to join her during a live performance. They may have flatlined, but the status quo seems curiously unchanged.

I think I'm a pretty useful member of society. I knock out words, articles, blogs, books. I create. But I'm a sad-ass somnambulant snail compared with these pulseless workaholics. Why do I even try when I'm getting lapped by corpses? Please folks, give it a rest.

QUADRABOOB & UNIBOOB

PUNCH RATING 👊 👊

Any sort of ill-fitting bra on myself or anyone else chaps my hide (particularly around my chest). Just like jeans that are too small, the wrong fit will give you a muffin top up top—not a tasty look.

Quadraboob looks terrible and feels even worse. Are two breasts not enough for you? Do you need to one-up (or two-up) the rest of us by stuffing yourself into a cup size so small that your bodacious boobies spill up and over, clearly trying to

> **FACT OF THE MATTER**
> ✦ It's not rocket science: Circumference of torso over the fullest part of your tits minus the circumference of torso directly under the breast = cup size (1 inch per cup; e.g. 3 inches = C cup)

escape their Lycra vise? Like wishing for unicorns or a certain Fitzwilliam Darcy, wanting to be a 34C doesn't make it so.

Then there's the uniboob, which, if you haven't had this mammary treat thrown in your face, occurs when you stuff your junk into a tight bra bandage so that you get one lump sum across your chest. Sure, the girls will be immobilized during a workout, but this ta-ta tube will also look like you're squirreling away a loaf of bread or a salami in your shirt. While delicious, they sure can't compare with your luscious décolletage.

Beeline to your nearest lingerie department and get fitted. Yes, you may be a size larger than you thought, but if you keep smothering and smashing and shoving your breasts into a compression bandage, I'm going to have to fill an over-the-shoulder boulder holder with an actual boulder and knock some sense into you.

RENAISSANCE FAIRES

PUNCH RATING

As the weather warms up, my thoughts naturally turn to sunscreen, outdoor cinema, beach vacations…and, unfortunately, Renaissance faires. From meadow to wood, these traveling minstrel shows set up shoppe for a few days of costumed frivolity. Celebrating the age of the Bard, Ren Faires provide a balm to the spirit, a respite from the modern storm, a step back in time, a rare opportunity to rub starched linen elbows with the occasional jongleur.…

In other words, these most rare and precious of gatherings are a time to inflict some serious old-school torture.

Ye Olde Newsflashe: If you're carrying a lute, you clay-witted codpiece, you're gonna get your ass kicked. The Dark Ages may be over but I'm still going to make your world go black. To aid me in my quest, I call upon my noble and true hand puppet. With mini club in hand, Punch can swing away in the direction of your jingly jester hat. With a heavy tankard, he can swipe at wenches and whelps in kind. This is one Renaissance man I can get behind.

Verily.

> **FACT OF THE MATTER**
> ✦ Most Ren Faires are set during the reign of Queen Elizabeth I, the height of the English Renaissance; curiously, few to none are set during the actual Italian Renaissance.
>
> **FACT OF THE MATTER**
> ✦ We have the Renaissance Pleasure Faire of Southern California to thank for all the merriment; it's regarded as the first modern Ren Faire, opening in 1962.

RESTAURANTS THAT DON'T PUT SALT ON THE TABLE

PUNCH RATING

I had the most amazing meal at the newest hot spot in town. Brick walls, warm candlelight, waiters with Ira Glass eyewear and corresponding attitude, hour-long waits. You know the place.

This time, the food lived up to the hype. We ordered the tasting menu, and soon a dizzying array of appetizers hit our table, followed by homemade spaghetti. Then came two entrees, one of which was pork cheeks, a dish that will dance through my dreams. Two desserts brought up the rear and went straight to my rear.

> **FACT OF THE MATTER**
> ✦ In France, many foodophiles keep small salt cellars on their person so they are always prepared to season...in a pinch.

All in all, a perfect evening.

Well, except for one tiny little thing that forced me to bust out a four-letter word: *Salt.*

Much like my personality, my palate runs toward the salty side. While I usually order dishes based on how the chef wants them prepared, I also want the right to season my food to my palate's preference. I wanted to sprinkle the bread with sea salt after I dip it in olive oil. I wanted to add a pinch to the bolognese sauce, which, while full of flavor, was a little too Healthy Choice for my taste buds.

But there was no shaker or cellar in sight. Like a napkin and silverware, salt on the table should be a given. Don't make me ask for it, and don't arch your judgmental foodie eyebrow at me when I do. While I may be rubbing salt in the wounded ego of Chef Fancy-Pants, it's definitely preferable to punching you where your taste receptors don't shine.

SCRABBLE

PUNCH RATING

I suck at Scrabble. I mean, I suck dead bear dry. I don't know if I get too caught up in trying to wow everyone with an OED-worthy word. Maybe I'm fixated on the triple-word score. Whatever the case, I get a serious ass-whupping every time, usually by a seventh grader or a great-grandparent.

I want to punch Scrabble and its smug ten-point Z tiles right where it counts—namely those 101 two-letter words—because they are a reminder of how inept I am. I like to avoid humiliation at all costs, so why would I belly up to the coffee table and let my friends and family in on

> **FACT OF THE MATTER**
> ✦ Architect Alfred Mosher Butts (total letter score: twenty-eight) created the game in 1938, figuring out the distribution and points of each letter based on a frequency analysis of letters from such sources as the *New York Times*.

the fact that my English degree was a waste, along with that dictionary I got for my 16th birthday? What good is it knowing big words when I get routinely trounced by xi, qi, and do re mi?

I may not get the triple-letter score, but I do have a five-fingered fist that will produce a five-point word. In a word, OW.

SEAT HOGS

PUNCH RATING

After suffering through planes, trains, and automobiles, I've had it with all the greedy fucks who ooze over several seats. At the airport, businessmen ignore the masses at the jam-packed gate and set up shop with their computer and carry-on to one side, meal to the other, and cords snaking out and plugging up all the available outlets.

On the bus, selfish hosebeasts sit on the aisle, cock blocking the empty window seat next to them by dumping a backpack on it, or simply ignoring my presence behind sun-blocking shades or the pretense of sleep. And don't get me started on the male leg spread on display on the bus or subway—your penis isn't that big and no, you don't need to air out your junk.

If you insist on being a waste of space, I'm afraid I have no choice but to assume the seat of power and hand your ass to you on a silver platter. You'll feel the earth move under your feet as I herd you to a standing-room-only area for the duration of your trip. If you covet your neighbor's seat again, I'm going

> **FACT OF THE MATTER**
> ✦ Gordon Gekko famously said, "Greed, for lack of a better word, is good." And you see how well that worked out for him. So pick up your ratty messenger bag and move yo' greedy ass.

to gather up your belongings, pile them in your lap, and wrap you in yellow "POLICE—DO NOT CROSS" tape. That should contain you nicely while I punch your greedy gob. Awake now? No? Then you won't feel it when I smother you with your travel pillow.

SHOELESS HOUSEHOLDS

PUNCH RATING

Increasingly, when I enter someone's home, I'm shoehorned into a foyer lined with shoes and instructed to add mine to the pile.

Um, I came for a party, not for a pedicure.

I get that folks don't want their hardwoods scratched and scuffed by my stilettos. I understand that paranoid parents are afraid of the germs that I'm tracking in on the soles of my shoes.

Call me a heel, but I don't want to walk around in my socks or bare feet. My shoes deserve to be seen as God and Christian Louboutin intended: on my feet. And without the boost of the heel I am never without, my jeans sweep the floor. From my POV, this has only one bright side: My friends' floors never need to be mopped. My pant legs and socks do it for them.

> **FACT OF THE MATTER**
> ✦ According to the Janka Ball Rating system, Brazilian Cherry is the hardest wood for flooring, so fork over the extra cash for your hardwood floors and let guests keep their shoes on.

If people keep demanding that I kick off rather than kick up my heels, I am going to kick them in the face—right after I shuffle around their house with 80-grade sandpaper taped to my feet.

SIDEWALK HOGS

PUNCH RATING

When people ask me if I'd rather have the superpower of invisibility or flight, I always go with flight.

Apparently, I'm already invisible.

At least it seems that way when I'm strolling through my neighborhood and spy two or three chuckleheads walking toward me. Talking to each other, they don't give up an INCH of space. They don't acknowledge my existence. They wouldn't know if I was tricked out in fetish gear or pointing a flamethrower directly at them. As these fuckers approach, it becomes a game of sidewalk chicken, and I always lose. At the last minute, I veer out of their way, usually tripping into a tree bed or slamming into a building.

No, excuse *me*.

Far be it from me to interrupt, disturb, or derail you, you self-absorbed dickwads with crapass peripheral vision.

Let's not forget about the

> **FACT OF THE MATTER**
> ✦ The average width of a sidewalk is six feet, plenty of room for you and your friend or stroller to let me pass, so move yo' ass.

strollers. I frequently dodge mommies and strollers who greedily spread out across any available paved surface. Believe me, I understand these gals' need to get some sun and girl talk. But let me tell you, they are tough mamas. Infantry units can use these chicks on their front lines, as they never break formation. I can practically see the tumbleweeds as I stare down a fence of Bugaboos and estrogen at high noon. Of course, I wind up looking like a total dick when I try to break on through to the other side.

It's time to take action! I'm staging a silent protest, and I'm asking you to join me. When you encounter a line of people coming at you, stop. Stand still. Break their synchronized stride and make them flow around you. You can pick up the pace after these wastes of space walk on by. If they bump into you, well, I think you know what to do. You saw *The Karate Kid.*

Sweep the leg.

SILK FLOWERS

PUNCH RATING 👊 👊 👊

Mom, commenting on the décor of the trailer she bought in Texas for the winter months: "My goll, you should have seen this place when we bought it. It was filled with rag-nasty plastic flowers."

Me: "Ugh, I hate those. I mean, what's the point?"

Mom: "Yeah, I threw them out and replaced them with some really nice silk flowers."

Me: "Uh…."

I love that my mother sees a marked class difference between plastic and silk flowers. To me, they are all the same: fake, non-fragranced doodads I have to dust. Why clutter up your home with bouquets of immortal meh?

I realize you may not be home long enough to keep a plant alive or you have a black thumb or you can't afford to buy cut flowers very often or your cat could die if he chewed on a lily, but here's my question: Why do you need anything at all? If you like the look of flowers, just get a print of some sunflowers or put a daisy magnet on the fridge. Don't clutter up the place with phony ferns and bogus pots of orchids.

> **FACT OF THE MATTER**
> ✦ Most fake flowers on the market are not silk—they're polyester. Whatever the case, rest happy in the knowledge that both types are treated to be flame retardant.

Nip these faux-ers in the bud and leave them where they belong: in a retail garden (i.e. Michaels, aisle 7).

SPECIAL-OCCASION FLEECE

PUNCH RATING

As the curtains opened on my evening, things looked promising. I bellied up to the bar, where I was greeted by a handsome man in a natty suit. We moved on to the theater to see a brand-spanking-new comedy.

> **FACT OF THE MATTER**
> ✦ Perhaps I'm being too hard on humbly dressed theatergoers. In Shakespeare's day, a good portion of the audience comprised groundlings, poor working-class stiffs who would have killed for a pair of Crocs or a polarfleece.

There was, however, one slight hitch. Actually, there were a few hundred hitches surrounding me. Men and women alike were sporting fleece vests, cargo shorts, baseball caps, polo shirts adorned with Microsoft logos, and grotty comfort sandals. The audience looked like they were ready to gut a fish, not watch a performance by professional actors (that they paid good money to experience).

Like weddings, job interviews, and black-tie galas, the theater is a special event. Like spotting a unicorn or rainbow, it's not something that happens every day, at least in my world. The theater is a reason to get dressed up, not *give* up. Akin to wearing pajamas as outerwear, wearing convertible pants and a hoodie is a sign that you don't care, either about yourself or the cultural institution. I know I live in Seattle, but would it kill you to wear tinted lip gloss or pants that reach to the floor? If you keep insisting on wearing the same garb for weeding the garden and supporting the arts, I'll have no choice but to bring the lights down on your sorry performance. And... *scene.*

SPINNING BEACH BALL

PUNCH RATING

My computer is on its last legs, I get it. I don't have to hear the death rattle to know its days are numbered. But yet my MacBook has to keep reminding me that it's a hunk o' junk. In fact, it throws it in my face in the form of an obnoxious beach ball that frolics all over my screen, mocking me and my three-year-old equipment.

Apparently, my rotten Apple can't keep Word from quitting on me but it can still muster up the energy to flip me the rainbow bird.

> **FACT OF THE MATTER**
> ✦ Before Apple's "spinning wait ball," there was a wristwatch that appeared on the screen when everything else froze on the screen. It was equally aggravating.

I hate to wait to begin with. Throw the spinning Trivial Pursuit pie into the mix and you have a serious suck cocktail. Since baby needs to write, I have to resist the urge to punch my laptop in its smug but increasingly ineffective LCD face. But on the rainbow brite side, while I wait for the beach ball to get its yayas out, I have ample time to think about how I'm going to burst this trouble bubble when I finally upgrade.

STAYCATIONS

PUNCH RATING

This has been the era of the "staycation," a dumbass euphemism for being too broke to go anywhere interesting. Instead, people are encouraged to discover their own town, to go on holiday in their own backyard—literally, their own backyard. Instead of flying to a foreign country, renting a condo at the beach, or roadtripping to Wall Drug, set up a tent on your patio and sleep al fresco. What could be better?

Um, most anything.

If you are sitting on your couch for two weeks, you're not on vacation. You're unemployed or broke or both. Vacationing at home only makes you think about the shit you have to get done. Instead of recharging your batteries on this naycation, you'll paint the kitchen, record your expenses into Quicken, grout the tub. Some holiday.

It almost beats that time when you were 11 and you went on that last cross-country family roadtrip before your parents split up, doesn't it?

Naming it something annoyingly cute doesn't make it so.

> **FACT OF THE MATTER**
> ✦ "Staycation" was added to Merriam-Webster's Collegiate Dictionary in 2009, proving once again that the Oxford English Dictionary is the way to go.

Just look at Soleil Moon Frye or the critter from Gremlins. Yeah, Gizmo was darling…until you added water. A staycation sounds appealing…until you realize that you just reorganized your closet, waxed the floors as well as your bits and pieces, and sewed all the missing buttons on your clothing. Productive? Yes. Relaxing? Just stay no.

Don't even get me going about babymoons….

STEAMPUNK

PUNCH RATING

I like imagination. I like creativity. I don't like this Victorian goth take on the Renaissance Faire. Instead of a jongleur in a jester's cap, steampunkers strap on leather goggles and embrace a good Rube Goldberg machine or Tesla coil for shits and giggles.

The thing is, as Billy Joel would say, the good old days weren't always good. If you're going to fire up some steam-powered contraptions using your erector set, you'd best showcase the tuberculosis and smallpox that rocked 19th-century Britain as well.

> **FACT OF THE MATTER**
> ✦ The Steampunk World's Fair debuted in 2010, an annual event attracting masses of leather-goggled knobs to that hotbed of steam-powered innovation, New Jersey.

You aren't edgy or alternative. You're just a former LOTR/Star Wars/D&D fan dressed up as an H.G. Wells wet dream. Doff the leather waistcoat and travel back to the present before I engage in a little time travel of my own and sic a Morlock on you.

STRIPPER BROWS

PUNCH RATING

I really have to draw the line. Pencil-thin brows and sperm brows don't belong on the face. Put those sad things in a sterile cup where they belong.

I admit it: I plucked the fuck out of my eyebrows in seventh grade in an unfortunate experiment during a boring weekend. It was around the same time that I tried cutting my own bangs. Add to that a bad perm and you've got a whole lot of not-pretty going on. I tried to take some artsy shots, and since they were a bit out of focus, I looked a bit like Marlene Dietrich. Oh, who am I kidding? I looked like nine miles of bad road.

I digress.

Over the past couple of years, I've been letting the brows grow in while simultaneously watching a whole lot of reality TV. Invariably the skank shows are riddled with crippled eyebrows. Some are drawn on in a thin line (see Pam Anderson or John Waters' mustache).

Then there are the cock-tweezers trying to rock sperm brows. You know the kind: They start out sort of full and then they quickly taper to a thin tadpole tail. Is this an announcement that their hoo-hah is open for business? And if the sperm shape isn't bad enough, the over-plucked brows often start somewhere over the pupil instead of the inside corner of the eye, so these dumbasses already look punched in the face and vaguely surprised.

What's the deal? Are these brow-challenged chicks OCD and can't leave them alone? Do they have trichotillomania, working out their issues by pulling out their brows? Are they a living tribute to the comma?

Rather than punching these douchettes in their already damaged faces, I think a bit of hot wax is in order. Avoiding the eyebrow area, I think I'm going to treat you to a full facial wax, since you clearly like depilation so fucking much. And FYI, the standard tip for services rendered is fifteen to twenty percent.

FACT OF THE MATTER

✤ Beware the overplucking! If you ever decide to embrace your inner Brooke Shields, you might be out of pluck. Excessive plucking or waxing can make the hair follicle smaller or even damaged, meaning they may grow back smaller, finer, or not at all.

SUNGLASSES ON THE FOREHEAD

PUNCH RATING

If you haven't figured it out by now, I'm pretty fucking persnickety.

Admittedly, this may have something to do with the fact that I'm single, but I stand by my gripes. And one well-trodden irritation is the guy who wears his sunglasses on his forehead. Not the top of his head, mind you, but just above his eyebrows.

When I see this optical billboard advertising a blue-collar, blue-blocking frat boy, I can't see straight. I should turn a blind eye to such a small thing, but it drives me bananas.

Are you too lazy to hinge your shades to the top of your head? Have you converted your Cro-Magnon brow ridge into a

> **FACT OF THE MATTER**
> ✦ Also annoying, Croakies were first used by contractors and fishermen—you know, people who were worried about losing their glasses. In short order, the sunglasses strap was co-opted by frat guys everywhere, giving me yet another reason to steer clear of the Sigma Chi house.

portable ledge for your Ray-Bans? Are you trying to shield your five-fingered forehead or receding hairline from harmful rays?

My only hope is that you wind up with an awesome tan line.

Equally as bad: Oakleys hanging off the nape of your neck. I'm looking at you, Guy Fieri, and not through rose-colored glasses.

TALKING ABOUT ONESELF IN THE THIRD PERSON

PUNCH RATING 👊 👊 👊 👊 👊

"**I**'m bored of Bono and I am him—I'm sick of me. I felt it was a little limiting to be in the first person," Bono once said. I'm sad that I'm limited in the ways that I can punch him in his pompous face.

My shit is royally irked when someone starts talking about him or herself in the third person. Politicians like Bob Dole and Joe Biden and athletes like Shaq and the Rock have been serving up illeisms for a long time. Yeah, I can smell what the Rock is cooking and it smells like dumbass, with a side of hubris. Are you royalty? A dead celebrity?

I think the only people allowed to refer to themselves in the third person are Steven Hawking, Mr. T, and the Hulk.

> **FACT OF THE MATTER**
> ✦ "Illeism" is the act of talking about yourself in the third person. By the transitive property, it is also the act of being a massive tool.

And oh yeah, Jesus, Buddha, and their pals. That's it, and even then they are walking a fine line between acceptable and my fist. I have found what I'm looking for, Bono, and it's your face.

TED TALKS

Have you noticed something spreading?

Nope, it's not the measles. It's the proliferation of TED Talks here, there, and everywhere. As well as that sentence, snuggled between the bizspeak and the chitchat: "Did you see that amazing TED Talk?"

When the TED conference series was launched in 1990, I loved the idea of talks on technology, entertainment, and design, but like *New Yorker* cartoons, I didn't know if they were for me. They were heady and mind-blowing, catnip to the NPR-totebag-carrying, interesting-eyewear-wearing crowd. I knew these video vitamins were good for me, but they were sometimes hard to swallow.

> **FACT OF THE MATTER**
> ❖ The most popular TED Talk of all time is Sir Ken Robinson's talk on how schools kill creativity, with thirty-one million views and counting. "We are educating people out of their creativity," Robinson says. And maybe TED is educating people right out of their spare time.

Then TEDx happened. Talks sprouted up everywhere, and I couldn't keep up. I can barely keep up with *This American Life* episodes, WTF podcasts, and all the shit queued up on my DVR, what with my job and all. How was I going to be able to watch ten- to twenty-minute videos on how to use a paper towel and bands that make their instruments out of vegetables?

Does every cul-de-sac have ideas worth spreading or, more importantly, ideas worth my time? I'm thinking no. For every Brené Brown talk that truly changes your thinking, there's a talk about the importance of ticking off your bucket-list items. Nice idea, but I can listen to a Tim McGraw song for that, and that only takes 4:27 of my life, allowing me to step away from my laptop and toward *actual* bucket-list activities.

TOMS

I'm not the best at seeking out charities to support, so I love the passive philanthropy of buying a pair of Warby Parker glasses or a pair of TOMS shoes. For every pair I buy, someone in need gets a pair. Great idea.

Then I went shopping.

TOMS classics are fug, a clumsy hybrid of Vans and those $8 Chinese black Mary Jane slippers we bought in the '80s. They have no arch support or style to speak of. The company has branched out into more fashionable styles like wedge sandals, so good on them.

But the people who wear TOMS act like they are part of some secret handshake club, that they like fashion but care even more about "giving back." Please, you just paid $68 for a pair of cloth slippers.

Rather than display your badge of honor on your Achilles heel, why not just donate the money you were going to spend on those shoes to one of TOMS' giving partners or your favorite charity? I don't need to humblebrag about my ethical shopping conduct. I'd rather just give the money to Heifers International than wear these walking ads to shoddy style.

> **FACT OF THE MATTER**
> ✦ As of press time, TOMS sells shoes, glasses, coffee, diaper bags, clothes, and other accessories, working with 100 giving partners to deliver TOMS shoes, sight, water, and safe births to those in need. Talk about an overachiever.

TOPPING OFF COFFEE WITHOUT ASKING

PUNCH RATING

I may be at my favorite watering hole, but I don't want to be watered. I just want to wilt into my chair and relax with a cuppa joe. Everything's coming up roses—until a constant gardener comes out of nowhere and tops off my mug with fresh coffee.

I spring to life.

I had just, finally, after much trial and error, gotten my decaf to the right temperature and the perfect hybrid of cream and sugar. When my guard is down

> **FACT OF THE MATTER**
> ✦ Caffeine can trigger GI issues, and it gives me gas, not what I'm going for in public, so please back away from my coffee cup.

(i.e., I'm eyeballing the hunky chef), regular joe splashes down into my cup, turning it back into the color of dirt.

Color me irked. I know you're trying to be proactive, but you're presumptive. No, I don't need any more coffee. Nope, I don't need it at a boil. Besides, you aproned Einstein, I was drinking decaf, not regular. Here's a tip: Ask me what I want. I just might warm up to you. Continue to go rogue and I'll just have to plant my fist in your face and stunt your growth.

TWENTY-MINUTE COFFEE PREP

PUNCH RATING

I don't know what's going on back there, but this isn't the Manhattan Project. It's a flippin' cup of coffee. While your coffee contraption looks like it was made by Skynet, I'm pretty sure it's not going to enable time travel. And it sure as hell isn't going to help me get back the twenty minutes I've been waiting patiently by the sugar station. What it—and you—are doing, however, is terminating my patience.

You don't need to take the scenic route to get to my drink destination. Really. Just jump on the espressoway and knock that shit out. Don't wax rhapsodic about your special blend that was picked by monkeys on the north face of a mountain in Colombia. Don't spam me with your disdain for my decaf order. And while I appreciate your java jive, I don't need or want you to craft a flower or devil or my silhouette in my cappuccino's microfroth.

> **FACT OF THE MATTER**
> ✦ The first espresso machine was patented in 1884 by Angelo Moriondo. I bet his patent arrived sooner than my latte order.

And when you take that long, you're setting up unreasonable expectations. If I don't have an orgasm on my first foamy sip, your fine art of grinding, steaming, and frothing is lost on me. And that's truly a shame.

TYPING EMAILS IN ALL CAPS

PUNCH RATING

When you rip off an email to me using only capital letters, I reckon that you're pissed, lazy, or both. You're pretty much passive-aggressively shouting at me. I'm certainly screaming inside my head reading your rant.

STOP IT.

I'M NOT KIDDING.

I'm a big believer in proper grammar and punctuation, and I feel there's a perfect word or phrase to express every thought or feeling. You don't need to resort to all caps to get your point across. I GET IT!

I also get that you're a monster A-hole who's in serious need of an etiquette class. I don't care that you're rushed, I don't want to hear that your pinkies can't operate the shift key properly, and I really don't give a shit that your hide is chapped. If you want to communicate with me, I'd better see some ascenders and descenders coming at me

> **FACT OF THE MATTER**
> ✦ Design guidelines often discourage using all caps for anything more than short headlines, as it reduces the shape contrast of words and makes them more difficult to read. Ascenders and descenders offer visual cues.

through my inbox. If there's no x-height to be found, you can bet money that I'm going to seriously font you up and put a cap in your ass, where it belongs.

UNSALTED NUTS

PUNCH RATING

Auntie Mame wisely observed, "Life's a banquet and most poor suckers are starving to death!" Well, I'd amend that to say that today, life's a banquet and most poor suckers are eating unsalted nuts on their way to their CrossFit class.

Like a dinner roll, nuts are a vehicle for something else. Rolls need to be buttered, and my nuts need to be salted. Come to think of it, my buttered rolls need to be salted, too.

These days, many diets sing the praises of nuts, saying they are great sources of protein and energy. So I snack. Trader Joe's trail mixes, almonds, pistachios—these all have a place in my laptop or workout bag. But whether or not I'm sweating out the sodium and electrolytes, I need salty nuts. Yes, I meant to say that. Salt in any form is necessary to enjoy a handful of toasted pecans or a schmear of almond butter.

Eschew the raw cashew and unsalted pistachio. They may provide fuel, but so do packets of GU energy gel and you don't see me squeezing that stuff into my gob, do you? I want to enjoy every single thing I put into my mouth, not munch on boring, flavorless nuts in the name of health. I may be fit, but unsalted nuts make me sick. I'm bringing some flavor back into my life, one honey-roasted peanut at a time.

> **FACT OF THE MATTER**
> → When did salt get such a bad rap? It supports thyroid function and balanced hormones, encourages a fast metabolism, maintains the body's pH level, improves sleep. And tastes so, so good.

UTILIKILTS

PUNCH RATING

Is a Tolkien convention in town, or are the Highland Games looming? Sorry to be a Utilipill, but Jesus, Mary, and Joseph, these man-skirts are fecking dumb. Unless you're heading to a Gathering in your clan's tartan, back away from the Utilikilt. Scotsman Alan Cumming can pull off a kilt when hanging at a gay bar or anywhere else. Ewan McGregor can sure as hell make it work. You can't.

What's that, you say? You're hot? Wear some cargo shorts. Edgy? Get a tat. *Lord of the Rings* fan? Move back to the shire, or at least New Zealand. Need a place to stick your tools? I can suggest a few alternatives.

> **FACT OF THE MATTER**
> + Utilikilts have only been around since 2000; the first one was created from a pair of military pants so the founder could tinker with his motorcycle more comfortably (i.e., ventilate his junk).

If you insist on never giving up your freedom, I'm going to give you some serious Maclovin'. I'll wrap my arms around your waist and reach for your big tool—namely, your ball-peen hammer. Cue the bagpipes, MacDeath, and get ready for a *Braveheart*-worthy beatdown. And if you persist in your questionable fashion choices, I'll have no choice but to pull out a dirk and go for the Utilikill.

And no, I don't want to see what you've got going on under there.

VANITY PLATES

PUNCH RATING

Personalized license plates are NOTSOGR8 in my book. In fact, IH8EM. The vehicular equivalent of the tattoo, they ask you to figure out what sort of six- or eight-letter phrase you're going to slap on your SUV's ass to define yourself. *Seinfeld*'s ASSMAN is ASSIN9, in my humble opinion. A lot of the plates are pretentious and blowhardian in nature (0-60IN4 or WISHURME), some—clearly owned by Stifler's peeps—are downright grody (8 ER OUT? Really, Illinois? Really?). There's a ginormous motor home sporting "GLBL WMR" which should really say "I M PRBLM." Some unoriginal chuckleheads are using online acronyms—if you are ROTFL, who's driving the car? I'm not rolling on the floor, dude. I'm right behind you, willing myself not to rear-end your metal tramp stamp.

My friends in Delaware will pay upwards of five figures for a rare black low-numbered plate. They view it as an investment and a status symbol. This sort of boggles my mind, especially when they tell me how much the single-digit plates go for (the number "6" plate went for $675,000 in 2008). What kind of vehicle deserves to host that sort of marquee plate? Is there a place for it on Air Force 1's vertical stabilizer?

> **FACT OF THE MATTER**
> ✦ The Commonwealth of Virginia may be called the "mother of presidents," but it might also be the "mother of jackholes"—it has the highest percentage of vanity plates in the nation.

I suppose a vanity plate is a way to show off without shelling out buttloads of clams. There is one plate that I can get behind, both on and off the road. A hearse's plate that reads "U R NEXT." Yep, buddy, you are. Because I M GUNIN 4U.

WHITE PIZZA

PUNCH RATING

I feel the same way about white pizza as I do about white chocolate and white-bean chili.

In a word, *imposter*.

White pizza may be a big, round, tasty breadstick, but it's not pizza. I may not be Italian, but I've eaten a buttload of pizza during the course of *la mia dolce vita*. A perfect pizza, with a chewy crust, bubbling cheese, and a tangy tomato sauce, can cause me

> **FACT OF THE MATTER**
> + Here's my recipe for a respectable pizza sauce: two tablespoons extra-virgin olive oil; three to four cloves of garlic, crushed; one can San Marzano peeled tomatoes, diced or crushed; pinch of sea salt; pinch of hot pepper flakes. Add all ingredients to a skillet on medium to low heat and cook it down until it thickens. Season to taste. That's it. No excuse for white pizza ever.

to temporarily lose my mind, only to find it right next to an empty pizza box or tray. I have been known to hoover the whole thing, be it a thick Chicago-style pizza from Gino's East or a homemade jobber with a cornmeal-dusted crust and fresh sauce.

A white pizza, however, has never inspired me to do more than flip the page on the menu and order another carafe of chianti. I need some color in my life, and if I can't get it from my pizza, I'll just drink my dinner instead. I'm not saying it's not tasty, but when faced with a choice between a *pizze bianche* and a tomato pie, why would I ever choose the white one? Olive oil is an *oil*, not a sauce.

I call bullshit on white pizza.

WINDSOCKS

PUNCH RATING

Your windsock stays on my mind. In fact, it's burned into my retina. I've tried to consider the lilies of the field, really I have, but I can't. Because your giant rainbow windsock is spoiling, spinning, and polluting my view.

I already knew you were a Notre Dame fan, thanks to the bumper sticker, license plate frame, and leprechaun antenna ball on your PT Cruiser. I don't need to be reminded of your misguided love, because frankly, I couldn't care less. And like your unfathomable affection for the Fightin' Irish, I also don't give a rat's ass about your penchant for pirates, whales, or snowmen. Why do you feel the need to clog up your yard, porch, stoop, or front door with these garbage bags?

Do you keep your seasonal or themed windsocks in the garage next to the extra lawn gnomes, gazing balls, and inflatable snow globes? Since your windsocks are most likely flame retardant, I think the best way to clean house is to sew these polyester

> **FACT OF THE MATTER**
> ✦ Who knew? Windsocks are actually used at airports and chemical plants to indicate wind direction and wind speed; I suspect those ones don't sport flowers or leprechauns.

air condoms together, fill them with helium, and create a hot-air balloon that can transport them all back to hell, or at least to the local landfill.

YEAR-ROUND CHRISTMAS DECORATIONS

PUNCH RATING

As we move into spring, we—like Julius Caesar before us—are tipped off to beware the Ides of March. But I think we need to keep an eye out for the real killer: Christmas shit that hasn't been taken down by March.

The holidays are usually a disappointment, so why prolong the agony well into the new year? Do you enjoy jacked-up electric bills? Do you get some sort of sick satisfaction by turning your house into a giant nightlight for your cul-de-sac? Does the Christmas spirit live within you and your candy-cane cardigan 365 days a year? Are you simply a lazy fuck?

You took down the inflatable snow globe, you say? Shut your effin' elfin trap. You've still got a sleigh parked on the roof and a flocked tree peeking out of the picture window. You might as well stick a red-and-green sign in your front yard that says, "I deserve to get run over by a reindeer."

Whatever the case, let me spell it out: Strands of icicle lights, while I stomach them for a five-week period in November and December, are not mood lighting. Tinsel is not to be trifled with after the first week of January. Send the holiday sweaters packing. And above all, a Christmas tree, real or artificial, is not a houseplant. After the holidays, it's an eyesore.

If you let your figgy pudding freak flag fly year-round, here's how I'm going to join in your celebration. I'm going to repurpose the little drummer boy's snare drum and smash it over

your head. I might grind up a little mistletoe and slip it into your eggnog. And if your house looks like Santa's workshop and crocuses are blooming outside, I'm going fill your stocking with lumps of coal and get Kris Kringle on your ass. Ho, ho, ho, motherfucker.

YOGA PANTS

Ladies of the yoga-pants-as-streetwear persuasion: Don't get it twisted. You're just as bad as the pajamas-as-outerwear People of Walmart, except you have a 401K and a will to live. In fact, you live the hell out of your life. You'll sleep when you're dead.

Meanwhile, you're overscheduled and you don't want any-

> **FACT OF THE MATTER**
> ♦ Lululemon came by its perky name because founder Chip Wilson reputedly said that the Japanese have a hard time pronouncing the letter "L," and the extra effort they'd have to make to say Lululemon would be brilliant marketing...as is the fitness-tramp-stamp logo on the back of their yoga pants.

one to forget it. You're far too busy with carpools and important deadlines at your WFH consulting gig to bother changing out of your workout gear. Because, oh yeah, you work out. The yoga pants say so. You know your way around a Pilates reformer and can stay in crow pose for more than a minute in your hot yoga class. Yoga pants are your way of broadcasting that you—and your toned ass—are better than me.

Yoga pants and a messy topknot announce to the world that you're fit, body and SoulCycle. On the flip side, however, you might be of the yoga pants subset who wears them despite having never stepped foot in a yoga studio. You don't live the hell out of your life. You just live for an elastic waistband, bless your heart, and you're not quite ready to make the leap to maternity pants, the ones with the stretchy panel.

Regardless, if you insist on wearing yoga pants to go shopping or out to lunch or to a business meeting, then men should start wearing some OG David Lee Roth spandex action. Because, you know, everyone wants to see that, too.

ZUMBA

PUNCH RATING 👊 👊

I want to like you, I really do. But while it seems like a requirement to wear a sports bra and to oil your abs in order to join the dance party, Zumba is the fitness equivalent of mom jeans. With its caliente Latino beats, it signals that you are clapping your way into middle age with abandon.

It might also mean that you miss Jazzercise something fierce.

I get that you want something to give meaning to your fitness life. Ever since your neighborhood Curves closed and your Tae Bo VHS tape snapped, you've been keen to step up your cardio. And since you love shaking it to the Macarena and the Chicken Dance, this seems like a perfect Kinection.

But you don't need Dumba and your local community center. Rather, pop your Menudo cassette into your Walkman and just dance. That combo never gets old.

> **FACT OF THE MATTER**
> ✦ Colombia isn't just the home of Sophia Vergara and Pablo Escobar; Zumba was first conceived in Colombia in the 1990s by Alberto "Beto" Perez.

ABOUT THE AUTHOR

JENNIFER WORICK

is a nice person…really. She is the *New York Times*–bestselling author of more than twenty-five books, including *The Worst-Case Scenario Survival Handbook: Dating & Sex* and *Nancy Drew's Guide to Life*. Named one of the four funniest bloggers in the US by *Reader's Digest*, she's written on everything under the sun for national magazines and websites like *The Huffington Post*, *Allure*, and *Salon*. A former publishing executive, Jennifer offers talks and workshops to help aspiring authors get published through The Business of Books (bizofbooks.com), and she regales college audiences with side-splitting but informative slide-show presentations based on her popular books. She lives in Seattle. Learn more at jenniferworick.com.